SECRET SUSSEX RESISTANCE

1940 - 1944

Stewart Angell

MP Middleton Press

Cover pictures:

Upper left - A rare photograph showing four members of the Ringmer Patrol in uniform (Full patrol pictured on page 42)

Upper right - Former Firle Patrol Leader, Bill Webber, looks down the emergency exit of his patrols underground hideout.

Diagram of the Firle Patrol hideout.

Lower central - Inside the Stanstead Patrol hideout, looking towards its decaying entrance.

Published September 1996
First reprint October 1996
Second reprint December 1996
Third reprint May 1997
Fourth reprint June 2003
Fifth reprint September 2004
Sixth reprint December 2008
Seventh reprint September 2009
Eighth reprint November 2010

ISBN 978 1 873793 82 4

© *Middleton Press, 1996*

Design Deborah Esher

Published by
> *Middleton Press*
> *Easebourne Lane*
> *Midhurst, West Sussex*
> *GU29 9AZ*
Tel: 01730 813169
Fax: 01730 812601
Email: info@middletonpress.co.uk
www.middletonpress.co.uk

Printed & bound by I.J.Graphics, Guildford, Surrey GU2 9XW Tel: 01483 235222

To Kayleigh and Danielle
may all your dreams come true

ACKNOWLEDGEMENTS

I would like to gratefully thank the following ex. auxiliary unit members, without whose help I could not have compiled this book.

Denis Allman, Tom Carr, Alan Cooke, Colin Cooke, George Cook, Frank Dean, Sidney Dumbrell, Sidney Gaston, Jack Harmer, Les Hawkins, Alan Heaver, Burt Holmes, George Huxham, Eric Johnson, Jack Matthews, Frank Mayston, Joe Norris, Ronald Peel, Frank Penfold, John Richards, Dick Sharman, Tom Smith, George Thomas, Bill Webber, Harold West and Charley Woolmer.

Thanks to the many people who have given me information or assistance, they include the following:- Vivien Abbott, George Anscombe, Bill Ashby, David Baker, John Baker, Geoffrey Bradford, Cecil Burbridge, David Campion, Dorothy Dinnis, Ray Dinnis, Hilda Drewett, Helen Goodwin, Michael Griffiths, Nicola Iona, Ted Jemmett, Pat Knight, Michael Lock, Christopher Lock, Nora Mills, David Miller, Bill Mottram, Ana Nunes, Diana Owen, Dick Passmore, Philip Pye, Iris Rowe, Robert Scott, Jean Scragg, Robin Shepherd, John Steer, Dennis Thompsett, Harold Thompsett, Andrew Trangemere, Ken Turner, Beatrice Veness, George White, John Willett, Peter Wilcox and Frank Williams.

Thanks to my underground research team in the field, who were David J. Burton for giving me photographic advice, Lynda Budd for often holding the other end of the tape measure and Nick "the revs" MacCaskill for transportation.

My thanks also go to Jo for listening to the progress I was making whether she wanted to know or not! Many thanks to my Mum for giving me encouragement, advice and helping me financially when I really needed it.

Thanks to all the staff at Polegate Library for chasing up requests for seemingly unobtainable books and articles.

Finally many thanks to Beverley Thompson, Jennifer Tasker, Colleen Brown and especially Karen Hilton for all the various pieces of typing and re-typing of the original manuscript.

AUTHOR'S NOTE

I have had an interest in military archaeology for as long as I can remember. I am especially fascinated with the subterranean aspects of military installations. However, I was unaware that a 'British Resistance', with a network of underground hideouts, had existed during the Second World War until August 1992 when I came across a small mention of it in the informative publication 'Hailsham at War' (Hailsham History Group, Ed. George Farebrother). I soon found, from my own research, that this underground army was on a par with the famous French Resistance. Such was the secrecy surrounding the whole operation that even now, some 50 years after the war, little information has been released concerning the men who made up the many patrols around Britain. Having lived in Sussex all my life, my interest lies in the men who formed the units in this county. What follows is the account of these men and what they were prepared to do for this country had the Germans invaded here.

Stewart Angell
Underground Research in Sussex

! WARNING !

All sites are on
PRIVATE PROPERTY
and cannot be visited

****

CONTENTS

PART ONE: ORGANISATION AND TRAINING

1. The Home Guard Auxiliary Units   8
     Origins   8
     An organised resistance   9
2. Coleshill House   11
     Individual experiences   11
     Techniques for avoiding detection   12
     Patrol competitions   12
3. Tottington Manor   14
     The West Sussex Scout Patrol   14
     Hideout construction in West Sussex   15
     The East Sussex Scout Patrol   16
     Other Hideout Constructions   16

PART TWO: THE SUSSEX PATROLS

4. The Home Guard Auxiliary Units of Sussex   23
   East Sussex Patrols   24
     Abbot's Wood Patrol   24
     Map of Hideouts   25
     Ashburnham Patrol   26
     Bishopstone Patrol   27
     Broad Oak Patrol   28
     Cooksbridge Patrol   28
     Crowhurst Patrol   30
     Ditchling Patrol   30
     Firle Patrol   33
     Bill Webber's Diary   33
     Hellingly Patrol   36
     Icklesham Patrol   38
     Iden Patrol   39
     Ringmer Patrol   41
     Rodmell Patrol   43
   West Sussex Patrols   44
     Arundel Patrol   45
     Clapham Patrol   45
     Goodwood Patrol   45
     Hurstpierpoint Patrol   47
     Small Dole Patrol   48
     Staplefield Patrol   49
     Stansted Patrol   53
     Warningcamp Patrol   54
     West Ashling Patrol   55
     Wiston Patrol   56
     Patrol Statistics   57

PART THREE: THE THREAT OF INVASION

5. Operation Sealion   58
6. Life expectancy in the event of an invasion   59
7. Stand Down   60
8. Conclusion   61

APPENDIXES

A. Equipment   65
     Personal equipment and side arms   65
     Small arms   67
     Explosives   68
B. Related Organisations   73
     Special Duties Organisation   73
     East Sussex   74
     West Sussex   77
     Zero Stations   79
     Stand Down   83

BIBLIOGRAPHY

BIBLIOGRAPHY   84

MAP TO SHOW THE POSITION OF AUXILIARY UNIT UNDERGROUND HIDEOUTS THROUGHOUT SUSSEX

PLEASE NOTE: All hideouts are located on privately owned land, therefore access is prohibited.

KEY TO MAP PATROL HIDEOUTS

1	ABBOTT'S WOOD	555	038	15	CLAPHAM	111	065
2	ASHBURNHAM	682	168	16	GOODWOOD	928	086
3	BISHOPSTONE	491	021	17	HURSTPIERPOINT	284	142
4	BROADOAK	843	216	18	SMALL DOLE	204	080
5	COOKSBRIDGE	386	123	19	STANSTED	761	121
6	CROWHURST	760	130	20	STAPLEFIELD	279	222
7	DITCHLING	345	196	21	WARNINGCAMP	053	077
8	FIRLE	474	062	22	WEST ASHLING	820	108
9	HELLINGLY	604	123	23	WISTON - LOCATION UNKNOWN		
10	ICKLESHAM	862	145	24	WEST SUSSEX SCOUT PATROL MAIN		
11	IDEN	892	219		HIDEOUT	022	092
12	RINGMER	449	142	25	EAST SUSSEX SCOUT PATROL MAIN		
13	RODMELL	397	052		HIDEOUT	555	019
14	ARUNDEL	990	120	*	TOTTINGTON MANOR REGIONAL HQ		
					AND HIDEOUT	215	116

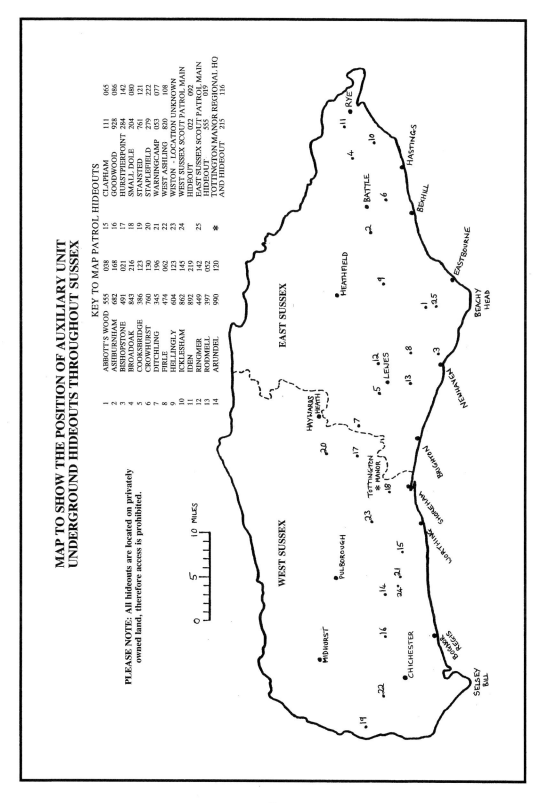

PART ONE

ORGANISATION AND TRAINING

1. THE HOME GUARD AUXILIARY UNITS

One of Britain's best-kept secrets of World War II was the Home Guard Auxiliary Units, which used the status of the Home Guard as a cover for their real activities.

The Auxiliary Units were formed into small, localised patrols all around the country. These, in effect, became the so-called 'British Resistance'. The excellent book '*The Last Ditch*', by David Lampe, revealed many of the secrets behind the auxiliary units, especially in Kent. However, there is no known written record of the Sussex patrols, either of their members or even of their existence. The author has endeavoured to locate, or document, all the original members of the Auxiliary Units. Unfortunately, due to the passage of time, there are inevitable gaps. In some cases, whole patrols have now died, and with them their memories.

The narrative that follows is the most comprehensive account of the members and activities of the Auxiliary Units of Sussex that is possible at this time. It is to be hoped that, in the future, the release of official documents relating to the Auxiliary Units will cast further light on this interesting period of our history.

Origins

The history of the formation of the Auxiliary Units is fascinating. They were an offshoot of Section D, which itself was founded in March 1938 as part of the Secret Intelligence Service. Section D's leader, Major Lawrence Grand, came from The Royal Engineers and had the task of assembling personnel to enforce its objective. This was to "investigate every possibility of attacking potential enemies by means other than the operations of military forces". Most of their work was conducted overseas. However, a (very disorganised) resistance was formed in this country, leaving explosives, small arms and food stores at various secret locations.

Only one of these early groups has come to light. It was formed around February/March 1940 and was based at the Star Brewery, Eastbourne. The four members of the group were Ronald Cardwell, part-owner of the Star Brewery, and three of his employees: Henry Scolater, the director/manager; Frederick Steer, the works manager; and Burt Hodsoll, a brewer. Each man had a revolver and the group had a store of explosives with time pencil fuses. They had a radio transceiver contained within a briefcase which was hidden in a secret compartment at the top of the brewery's water tower. Transmissions were made at least once a week. Many of these pre-war groups were disbanded when the next phase of the resistance was formed. However, the men at the Star Brewery remained operational till the end of the war, assuming an intelligence-gathering role.

After Operation Dynamo, the code-name for the evacuation of the British Expeditionary Forces from Dunkirk, it seemed that a German invasion of this country was to be expected. Consequently, a total re-think of the British resistance organisation was needed.

An organised resistance

In May 1940, Colonel Colin Gubbins formed a tightly-structured resistance that was to be supplied with the best weapons available and with modern plastic explosives. He named them the 'Auxiliary Units', a deliberately nondescript title. Everything about the Auxiliary Units was to be kept highly secret.

The following letter was sent to the Prime Minister, Winston Churchill, informing him of the progress made by 8 August 1940 in the formation of the Auxiliary Units, and describing how they were to be organised and trained.

SECRET

Offices of the War Cabinet
Richmond Terrace, Whitehall, S.W.1.

PRIME MINISTER

HOME GUARD - AUXILIARY UNITS

1. I think you may care to know of the progress which is being made in the or ganisation of the Auxiliary Units of the Home Guard.

Object

2. These Auxiliary Units are being formed with two objects:
    (a) They are intended to provide, within the framework of the Home Guard Guard organisation, small bodies of men especially selected and trained, whose role it will be to act offensively on the flanks and in the rear of any enemy troops who may obtain a foothold in this country. Their action will particularly be directed against tanks and lorries in lagger, ammunition dumps, small enemy posts and stragglers. Their activities will also include sniping.
    (b) The other function of the Auxiliary Units is to provide a system of intelligence, whereby the regular forces in the field can be kept informed of what is happening behind enemy lines.

Composition of Units

3. Units have so far been kept very small and consist for the most part of not more than a dozen men under a selected leader. Since their activities will usually take place under cover of darkness, it is essential that all members of these Units should be intimately familiar with the countryside. They are, therefore, largely being recruited from among farmers, gamekeepers, hunt servants and others who are particularly well acquainted with locality.

Equipment

4. The men are equipped with rifles and grenades and with a variety of other materials and devices, including delay action fuzes, plastic H.E. and incendiary bombs. In addition, it is hoped to issue them with a proportion of Tommy guns when these are available.

5. In order to enable them to carry out their second role, namely, to supply Home Forces with information of troop movements, etc. from behind the enemys lines selected units are also being provided with wireless and field telephone apparatus.

6. Moreover, certain areas where it is thought that they may be able to keep up their activities for a longer period, reserves of food and water are also being provided.

7. These stocks of equipment and food are being concealed in carefully prepared hide-outs, the whereabouts of which is known only to the local leader.

Command and Control

8. All the activities of these Auxiliary Units are under the direct supervision of Colonel Gubbins, who himself is on the G.H.Q Staff of Home Forces and are planned and carried out in the closest collaboration with the military authorities in the areas concerned.

9. Contact is maintained with these small scattered bodies through Intelligence Officers appointed for this purpose. There are 12 such officers on the establishment of H.Q. Auxiliary Units, and each is responsible for one of the areas shown on the attached map.
10. The duties of the officers are:
    (a) To form Auxiliary Units, selecting localities and personnel.
    (b) To distribute and conceal the special stores.
    (c) To train personnel in their duties and in the use of the special stores.
    (d) To act as liaison officers between the military Commanders and the Units.
11. In the event of invasion the Auxiliary Units will operate either on general instructions previously given, or if the situation permits, on the orders of the local Military Commander issued through the Intelligence Officer concerned.

Training

12. The training of the Units depends, of course, much upon the ability of the Unit Leader. However, all training is being personally supervised and directed by the Intelligence Officers, who are constantly touring their areas and who have the assistance of a small number of regular troops.
13. In addition, some very useful pamphlets on the use of explosives and on the the methods of guerrilla warfare have been produced in inconspicous covers for the instruction of the Units. I attach two of these pamphets as examples of the type of publications which are being issued.
14. From the above you will see that these Auxiliary Units, although only very recently formed, are going rapidly ahead, and should soon be in a position to give valuable help to the regular forces.
15. I think you will agree that they are doing well and deserve encouragement. With your permission, therefore, I would like to tell Home Forces that you attach importance to the work of this new branch of the Home Guard and are pleased with the progress made.

8th August 1940 D. Sandys

This letter mentions twelve intelligence officers enrolled by Gubbins to begin the operation. Each officer was given his own coastal area. He in turn selected junior officers, NCOs and other ranks as training personnel. They were then formed into scout patrols. One patrol was assigned to each intelligence officer, but, in the case of Sussex, two such patrols were formed.

Gubbins knew he needed local men to form the small patrols in each area, men who could be trusted and who had a good knowledge of their surroundings. He decided it would be best to obtain his resistance men from the Home Guard. Contrary to popular belief (mainly due to the BBC series 'Dad's Army'), the Home Guard was not totally made up of bungling old men. Many younger men who were in reserved occupations joined their ranks. This is not to say that every member of the Auxiliary Units was originally in the regular Home Guard. Potential members were always vetted by the local police before they were allowed to join. All the men had to sign the Official Secrets Act, and, on joining the Auxiliary Units, were issued with Home Guard uniforms bearing the number of their battalion. These battalions were: 201st in Scotland; 202nd in Northern England; and 203rd in Southern England. None of these battalions ever had official recognition, which meant they were not covered by the Geneva Convention. If the men were captured, they would have been shot. Hitler had already threatened the regular Home Guard with summary execution, if he invaded.

When a patrol was formed, it had to have its own underground hideout. This was known as an Operational Base or OB. The hideouts were to be used in the event of an invasion. They were well-hidden and purpose-built to house the patrol along with the necessary food, water, ammunition and explosives.

On invasion, the idea was that each patrol would let the Germans occupy their area, emerging at night to perform acts of sabotage on German installations. They were also to hamper the enemy's movements around the country by blowing up roads, bridges and railway lines. After an invasion, the patrols were thought to have a life expectancy of just two weeks.

2. COLESHILL HOUSE

In August 1940 it was decided that the Auxiliary Units needed to establish a base for their operations and training.

Coleshill House at Highworth, near Swindon, Wiltshire, was an ideal choice. This large 17th century house, within its own extensive grounds, was isolated enough to conceal its use as the headquarters of the Auxiliary Units. Training of auxiliaries took place mainly at the weekend. The men would be taught sabotage techniques and how to handle high explosives. This training, although basic, gave the men a solid knowledge-base on which to build with further training in their own local areas.

To prevent anyone infiltrating the top secret training at Coleshill, an unusual entry system was devised. Any men sent for training at Coleshill were told to report to Highworth Post Office. On arrival at the post office, the Post-Mistress would telephone Coleshill and simply tell them a parcel was waiting to be picked up. A vehicle would then be sent, and only when the identity of each man was verified were they taken back to Coleshill House.

Individual experiences

Two former auxiliaries recalled their time at Coleshill House. Joe Norris of the Ashburnham Patrol remembers going by car to Coleshill, with his patrol, for a weekend of training. This was a very intensive course which included lectures inside the house, followed by practical work outside. One such piece of practical work involved the men, in a dug-out surrounded by its own spoil, having to throw live grenades. One man threw a grenade which promptly hit a tree and bounced back onto the spoil. It exploded, half-burying the men in the dug-out. Luckily, no-one was injured.

Although the house was used for lectures, the visiting men were accommodated in various other buildings within its grounds. Joe Norris recalls arguing with fellow patrol member Eric Johnson about who was to sleep on the top bunk. One man, from a different area, who was supposed to attend on the

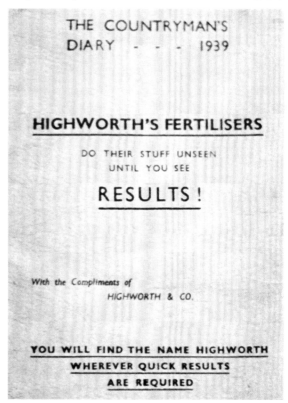

THE COUNTRYMAN'S
DIARY - - - 1939

HIGHWORTH'S FERTILISERS

DO THEIR STUFF UNSEEN
UNTIL YOU SEE

RESULTS !

With the Compliments of
HIGHWORTH & CO.

YOU WILL FIND THE NAME HIGHWORTH
WHEREVER QUICK RESULTS
ARE REQUIRED

1. The official auxiliary unit training manual disguised as 'The Countrymans Diary' - 1939. Highworths fertilisers no doubt refers to the explosives used by the auxiliary units. The quick results meaning not only the effectiveness of these explosives but also the efficiency of its users.

same weekend as the Ashburnham Patrol, ended up at another place called Coleshill, near Birmingham - not a good start to his Auxiliary Unit career.

Charley Woolmer of the Bishopstone Patrol remembers going to Coleshill by train, being picked up by an army vehicle and taken directly to Coleshill House. He too recalls lectures being delivered in a classroom atmosphere, followed by practical experience. No notes were taken at the time. Everything had to be memorised. He remembers sleeping in a barn in the grounds, whilst the officers giving the lectures all slept in the house. The only written information was contained in the official Auxiliary Unit sabotage manual. This had forty-two pages and was full of information on detonators and explosives, and how to combine them. The manual was disguised by having the title, 'Countryman's Diary 1939' printed on its beige cover.

Techniques for avoiding detection

Training was not confined to the use of explosives. The men were taught the importance of teamwork and that every patrol member should have a complete understanding of the task he was to perform.

Basic methods of avoiding detection whilst on patrol were also covered. The men were never to carry such items as documents, keys or a white handkerchief. They were to avoid cattle at all times, and to use the wind to their advantage. Special attention was given to the arts of moving silently at night and remaining perfectly still for long periods of time. Every man, regardless of his size or age, was taught unarmed combat.

Guidelines on how to behave inside the hideout were laid out for all patrols. Most of these were simply common sense. One concerned smoking: this was only allowed for ten minutes in every hour. Another important guideline related to the temperature inside the hideout. Anything over 65-75 degrees Fahrenheit was considered too hot.

Patrol competitions

An annual Home Guard Patrol Competition took place at Coleshill. Eliminating rounds were held in each county to find the best patrol to represent it in the prestigious final. The following letter, about the third such competition, was sent to all Sussex patrol leaders. It lists the events and how marks were to be awarded.

G.H.C. Home Forces
4th July, 1943

SECRET   Subject: Third Home Guard Patrol Competition
To:All Patrol Leaders.

   The third Home Guard Patrol Competition Semi Finals and Final will take place in October and November this year. Dates for area and County Finals will be notified later.   The six events are varied and the necessary training to ensure that a Sussex Patrol wins the shield will be arduous but interesting and am sure that all Auxiliers will give all their available spare time to attend regularly so that each patrol may work and train as a team.
The events are as follows:
Event 1. Mills Grenade Throwing. The target wil be the same as last year i.e. 10x10 enclosure of C.G.I. sheets on their sides, giving walls 2ft high. 12 Grenades will be thrown by each man, two from each of six pegs in different directions. Ranges will vary between 40yds and 15yds and the shorter ones may be marked kneeling or lying.   Standard unprimed grenades wil be used but the pins will not be pulled out. Bombs may not be lobbed underhand. Markings 1 point for each hit. Bombs landing short and bouncing in are misses, those landing inside and bouncing out are hits.
Event 2. Elementary Foot Drill. (See Appendix A)

Event 3. Miniature Rifle Practise - Grouping. Lying with wrist or forearm supported. 10 rounds per man. Range approximately 20 yards (Probably by artificial light). Rifles will be without telescopic sights and for Semi Finals and Final will be supplied by Coleshill. Scoring will be for group of best NINE shots. i.e. one wide will be allowed. 0.5...5pts. 1...3pts. 1.5...2pts. 2...1pt.

Event 4. Efficiency Race First man runs 5yds to to obstacle (either short length of Concrete Drain Pipe or two wooden arches 1 yd apart and 1ft high by 2ft wide) and crawls through. Runs 10yds to two Mills Grenades. One is whole the other stripped. Assembles latter and strips former. Runs 10yds to a 303 rifle and fires at a 2" x 2" target at 50 yds until he hits it. Runs 10yds to a revolver (alternative S+W and Colt will be provided) loads three rounds fires at full length figure target at 10yds until he hits it. Reloading three rounds at a time if necessary. Returns through obstacle. As soon as he is through 2nd man may start.

Event 5. Explosives - Appendix B 5 of 10 possible problems will be set by the Umpire. In addition a sixth will be set on the spot for the P.L. (No. [12] Appendix B).

Event 6. Daylight Patrol - Observer Exercise Six targets will be put in well separated areas. Each will consist of a number of small piles of petrol tine bearing a random number on top, facing four ways. Each pile to be within 20yds of the next. Each man is given a map on which the position of the dump is shown. Each area is guarded by a umpire with an orderly and sentry who remains near the target. Each patrol sends an observer simultaneously to each target area. Each observer tries to locate as many piles as posible proving that he has seen each by writing down its random number on a card. If seen by a sentry or umpire the orderly collects his card. Points awarded for each number correctly copied even if observer captured and double points for a safe return. Time limit 2.5 hours. Any form of sniper veil or suit may be worn.

NOTE: This event will probably take a modified in the County Final.

The training for events 1,3,4 and 6 can be carried out with little or no help from instructors but they will be available should you require assistance. My instructors will give the necessary preliminary training for events 3 and 5.

L.R. Bradford, Lieut. Scout Officer

Small Dole, 21.6.43.

2. Alan Cookes schedule for the final at Coleshill in 1943. The Icklesham Patrol became team 'A' after the draw on Friday evening.

3. Event 6 did indeed take a modified form in the final. Each team member was given a small map with a cross marked on it, signifying the point they had to reach. This is Alan Cookes map given to him just before the start of event 6. On its reverse is the letter 'A' indicating whose team it belonged to.

Sussex was represented twice in this annual competition by the Icklesham Patrol, according to all accounts a very accomplished team of men. The first time was in 1942, when they won the competition. Each patrol member received a one pint pewter tankard as memento of the occasion. Each tankard was simply inscribed with the word 'Winner', along with the year.

The following year found the Icklesham Patrol returning to Coleshill. Former patrol member Alan Cooke remembers the 1943 final. The Icklesham Patrol were up against patrols from Essex, Kent, East Lothian and Somerset. Alan Cooke recalls that his patrol always achieved a high score in the rifle practice and the lowest score for the foot drill. The competition was won by Kent, while Icklesham came second.

3. TOTTINGTON MANOR

Tottington Manor, at Small Dole in West Sussex, is described as a typical Sussex country manor house, and is currently used as a small hotel and restaurant. However, during the war, it was the regional headquarters for the Auxiliary Units in Sussex.

The Commanding Officer (known as the Intelligence Officer) was based here. The first CO was Captain J N W Gwynn. He remained in this position until October 1941. Then Captain C F G Bond took over until July 1942. The next CO was Captain R Benson; it is unknown how long he remained in this post, but he was certainly there in February 1943.

Also based at Tottington, but not quartered there, were the two scout patrols. These were made up of regular army personnel, one patrol to cover the east, and the other the west of the county. The scout patrol in the east was led by Lieutenant William Ashby, with thirteen men from the Queen's Royal Regiment under him. The western scout patrol was led by Lieutenant Roy Fazan, with thirteen men from the Royal Sussex Regiment. These patrols were used to help organise and assist in the localised training of each Auxiliary Unit patrol throughout the county. They remained at Tottington until February 1943, when they had to leave the Auxiliary Units to rejoin their regiments.

The West Sussex Scout Patrol

Two former West Sussex Scout Patrol members were interviewed: Sidney Gaston, a private, and Les Hawkins, a lance-corporal in the Royal Sussex Regiment. Les Hawkins remembers volunteering for the assignment, not knowing exactly what it was going to be, but hoping for an exotic overseas posting since, in order to be considered, the men had to be able to swim, fish and trap animals for food. On joining the scout patrol, all the men were briefed on the reason for its formation and sworn to secrecy. They were all promised that, at the end of this assignment, they could join elite sections of the armed forces such as the paratroopers, or become glider pilots.

The patrol was billeted two miles north of Arundel in the Rectory at South Stoke. The weathercock on the church still bears evidence of its use for target practice by various members of the patrol. Sidney Gaston recalls that each man was issued with a revolver, a fighting knife, a pair of rubber boots and a woollen hat. An unusual item of equipment, of which the patrol had around five between them, was a fold-up bicycle. This was made by Raleigh, having smaller-than-average wheels and a leather strap to enable the bike to be carried on a man's back when folded up.

Not only did the scout patrol train the various Auxiliary Unit patrols in West Sussex, but they themselves performed night-time mock attacks on such targets as the airfields at Tangmere and Shoreham, and the radar stations at Poling and Truleigh.

Hideout Construction in West Sussex

The scout patrol had three underground hideouts which they constructed themselves. Their first was built within a wood on Camp Hill, east of Amberley Station. It was made by sinking two narrow holes about fifteen feet apart, then picking out, by hand, the chalk in between these holes. Pat Darcy, another member of the patrol, who came from a mining background, was duly given this task. This method of construction left the surface undisturbed, helping to conceal its existence. All the chalk spoil had to be sandbagged and taken away into other parts of the wood to be dumped. It was then covered with leaves, moss and dirt so that it could not be seen from the air. The hideout measured approximately 12 feet long, 10 feet wide and just over 6 feet high. About half a mile to the west of the hideout was sited a small lookout, on the edge of a chalk pit. This took the form of a covered slit trench.

The second hideout was sited within the eastern part of Arundel Park, half a mile north of the Black Rabbit pub. This, according to Les Hawkins, was the deluxe version. It measured about 20 feet long, 10 feet wide and 8 feet high, with an emergency exit in the form of a thirty foot long concrete tunnel. The hideout was built by first digging out the hole, then putting in the main struts. These were made from locally-cut pine trees. The floor had a base of sand for drainage, topped with bricks. Next, 4 inch by 2 inch wooden battening was put all around the walls and wooden matchboard nailed to this. The roof was made up of wood and corrugated iron, with matchboard attached underneath to make the ceiling. The whole hideout then had four feet of soil on top of it. Entrance was gained by lifting a trapdoor and going down a set of brick steps. A car battery was used for electric light. Another lookout was positioned on the edge of a chalk pit just behind the Black Rabbit, giving a good view of the River Arun and the railway line. This section of line was a main target for the patrol in the event of invasion.

Their third hideout was built near Lavant, north of Chichester. Described by Les Hawkins as an oversized Anderson shelter, it was constructed much later on, about the middle of the war. The corrugated iron, he remembers, was especially thick. However, the overall size and exact location has been forgotten.

All three hideouts were intended to be used at the same time. The idea being that, after attacking the Germans in one area, the patrol would move on again. Extra supplies of ammunition, explosives and food were scattered around Sussex, concealed in underground hideouts. Two of these underground stores were sited in Rewell Wood, east of Arundel.

The following information has been supplied by Bill Mottram, who was a driver in the Royal Engineers during the war, and relates to one of the stores built in Rewell Wood. Bill Mottram had been part of the BEF and was evacuated from France a week after Dunkirk. He ended up in Newcastle and from there he was posted to Sussex because of his excellent knowledge of the county. Due to the threat of German invasion, all the signposts had been removed, making travelling around very difficult. As a driver, Bill Mottram's experience in negotiating the county's roads at night was put to full use. He was based at Bramber, West Sussex, and drove a team of four or five specialists (a carpenter, bricklayer, miner, painter etc).

The store was constructed around July/August 1940. At that time, various defence projects were being undertaken by the Royal Engineers and sometimes they started jobs but never finished them, or finished other people's work for them. Bill Mottram remembers driving the men to the construction site in Rewell Wood, carrying the building supplies for the day. They had a good stock of building materials at Bramber, particularly timber, because of all the buildings which the Royal Engineers had been demolishing around that area. The construction site was on the edge of Rewell Wood, and a camouflage net was used to disguise what was going on. The hole for the store was dug by hand, the chalk spoil being put into sandbags and later emptied below the trees in the surrounding area so that it could not be seen from the air. Once the hole was dug, the carpenters lined the walls and floor with timber. It is not known whether the roof was made from timber or corrugated iron. The store measured approximately 10 feet long, 8 feet wide and 8 feet high. They did not work constantly on the one site, so it took them about two weeks to finish. At the time of construction, none of the men building the hideout was told what it was going to be used for.

The East Sussex Scout Patrol

The scout patrol in the east of the county had at least two underground hideouts. One was sited within Beauport Park near Hastings, and the other within Holt Wood, Jevington. The latter measured 20 feet by 20 feet by 8 feet deep. It was built along the lines of an Auxiliary Unit hideout, having bunk beds and stores kept inside it. Although the hideout was only intended to be used by the scout patrol, a few East Sussex patrols knew of its existence. These men were told that they could use it as a refuge if they could not get to their own hideout, or if theirs had been discovered.

A few miles to the north, at Park Corner near East Hoathly, the patrol had an underground store containing additional supplies. After the two scout patrols returned to their regiments in February 1943, Sussex appears to have been covered by just one scout patrol. This was led by Lieutenant Roy Bradford of the 6th Battalion, Devonshire Regiment. His signature appears at the bottom of the above-mentioned letter of 21 June 1943, informing patrols of the Third Home Guard Competition at Coleshill. It is known that later on that year he was transferred to Devon, eventually becoming a member of the 1st Special Air Service Regiment.

Other Hideout Constructions

Tottington had various other personnel based there, such as a couple of drivers, two RAF radio operators, a full-time cook, Sergeant Heasman, who was a clerk in charge of the paperwork, and Sergeant Frank Mayston who was an explosives expert in the Royal Engineers Auxiliary Unit.

Frank Mayston related his involvement as a Royal Engineer with the Auxiliary Units at Tottington. He was a builder by trade, and became involved when he helped build the hideout underneath the so-called 'airship hole' in Kings Wood near Bilting in Kent. He was part of the team of Royal Engineers which included sappers from Hastings and Eastbourne. However, he never saw this hideout completed, as he was called back to Sussex halfway through its construction. This large hideout was intended to be used as a communal meeting point for any patrol members in Kent who were on the run. Compared to an ordinary patrol hideout, it was big, with enough room to sleep a hundred and twenty men, with food and water stores as well.

On his return to Sussex, Frank Mayston was made a full-time member of the Royal Engineers Auxiliary Unit, permanently based at Tottington. Initially, he and a few other men started building, mostly by hand, the hideouts for the Sussex patrols. They had very limited supplies of building materials, and usually used second-hand wood from other buildings, besides cutting down trees close to where construction was taking place. He remembers constructing the Ringmer and Cooksbridge Patrols' hideouts as well as the latter's lookout.

Tottington Manor had its own underground hideout. This was built by Frank Mayston and a few of his men, "in their spare time", as he puts it. Entrance was gained by sliding part of the cellar floor under the foundations of one of its walls. This section of the floor was, in fact, a piece of wood with the bricks that made up the floor cemented on top of it. After this was moved, it revealed a three foot drop. Beyond this, a 12 foot long passage led into the main room of the hideout. This room measured 12 feet by 12 feet and was 8 feet high. It would have contained the bunk beds, food stores and ammunition. There was a smaller, adjoining L-shaped room which was used as an explosives store and contained the Elsan chemical toilet. Leading off the main room, another passage carried along for about 12 feet, then made a right turn and continued on for another 8 feet, terminating at the emergency exit which was in the form of a 2 feet wide concrete tunnel. This tunnel is 43 feet long and runs out under the Manor's garden, with its exit disguised as a drain cover. It was built close to a row of existing drain covers, to help it blend in and disguise its true purpose. The hideout had electric lights and a water supply. Both of these were tapped from the Manor above. A primus cooker was built into one of the walls and had a washbasin next to it. In the event of an invasion, this hideout would have been used by the men based at the Manor.

They would have received information about German troop movements around the Tottington Manor area from either of the two underground lookouts which Frank Mayston and his men had dug on the Downs. One of the lookouts was half a mile to the south of the Manor, and gave a good view of the Manor and its grounds. This lookout had a direct telephone link with the hideout under Tottington. Laying the telephone wire was a major problem because of the Poynings to Small Dole road. This was solved by running it along a ditch at the edge of the road and putting it inside an existing pipe which ran under the road, to get it back to the Manor.

The other lookout was three miles to the east, and looked out onto the roads around Poynings. Both lookouts measured approximately 8 feet by 6 feet and were dug directly into the chalk, then lined with wood. Each would have had only one man positioned inside it, with a small amount of food and water. He would have noted down the details of the German troops and their movements. The nearest lookout would telephone the information back to the men in the hideout under Tottington. They in turn would have a good idea of targets they could sabotage at night, and what sort of equipment, such as explosives and detonators, were needed. The men in the lookouts would have been replaced every twenty four hours when possible, but it was thought that they could have been confined inside their small holes for anything up to a week at a time.

Tottington Manor was used for weekend training of the Sussex patrols, and inter-patrol competitions were regularly held there as well. Frank Mayston constructed an assault course in the grounds of the Manor for the purpose of night-time training. This included such obstacles as trip-wires, a rope over a pond and a chalk cliff hazard which had to be scaled. This course proved to be very popular with all the patrols. Although Frank Mayston was initially in charge of constructing various hideouts, he later went on to become an expert in explosives, the use of which he would teach to patrol members on training weekends.

He devised tests and compiled over 150 questions in the form of three quizzes, to help the men learn the many different techniques for using plastic explosives. He is still in possession of the quiz papers, and his official training manual which was issued at Coleshill House. This differed slightly from the 'Countryman's Diary' manual issued to the patrol

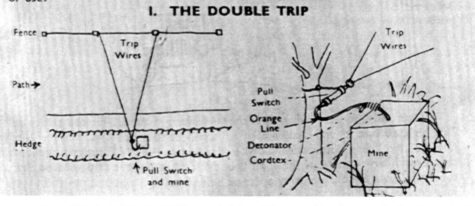

BOOBY TRAPS

All booby traps for our purpose must be simple and capable of being set up very quickly. The great majority will be outdoor ones and so some form of mine must be used to inflict casualties by shrapnel effect. If you do lay them indoors, 2 lb. of explosive will account for anyone in the average size of room. There will be no need for a mine, as the concussion will be sufficient.

The best booby trap is the one you invent yourself for your own local conditions—providing it is simple—but here are a few suggestions that may be of use:—

I. THE DOUBLE TRIP

4. The start of page 35 in the "Calender 1938" manual giving advice on making the most of using shrapnel within a booby trap.

5. Comical cartoon of a simple booby trap, showing a way of eliminating German despatch riders. No doubt, if used, would have been very effective.

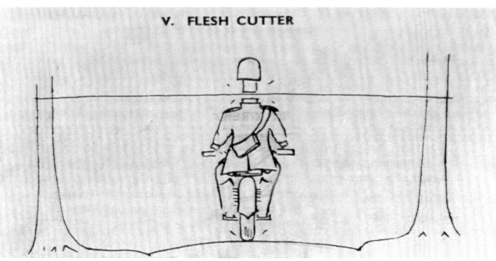

V. FLESH CUTTER

leaders. Its cover was green and only had 'Calender 1938' written on it. Inside, it had an additional seven pages, mainly covering several types of booby trap, including the anti-personnel (AP) switch. The AP switch is described as being a "self-contained booby trap of considerable nuisance value. When a man steps on it, a bullet passes through his foot and usually re-enters his person. It will also puncture motor tyres". This device, although available, was never used. The major drawback would have been recovering the unused switches. The preferred method of removal was to use a garden roller to fire them.

Frank Mayston would travel to Coleshill House every month to pick up fresh supplies of explosives which he brought back to be stored at Tottington Manor. These he delivered all over Sussex to each patrol as they were required. One use for the plastic explosive stored at the manor was for fishing! Apparently, only a small piece about the size of a golf ball was needed. After the explosive was thrown into the water, the shock waves from the explosion would stun the fish, which would rise to the surface and then would be fished out with a net.

The Manor had booby traps all over it in case invading Germans took it over. Various ingenious devices were used, such as hand grenades disguised as coal and left in the coal bucket by the fireplace, and cut-down bottles with candles in them which were in fact an explosive charge, the wick being the fuse. Green glass bottles were used so the charge could not be seen. Traps were attached to trip wires on cupboard doors and inside drawers. One rather sinister weapon, with which the men were all initially issued was a spiked knuckle-duster, but these were soon withdrawn.

6. The East Sussex Scout Patrol, Lieutenant William Ashby of the Queens Royal Regiment is sitting in the middle of the picture. Unfortunately none of the other members names are known however, they all belonged to the Queens Royal Regiment.

7. The West Sussex Scout Patrol. The back row from left to right:- Reg Vidler, Burt Libbiter (Royal Army Service Corps), Pat Darcy, Sidney Gaston, Ron Dodds, Bill Muschin, Gerald Savage (R.A.S.C.) and Jock Paul. Middle Row from left to right:- Jack Duffield, Les Kennard and Les Hawkins. Front Row from left to right:- Jack Dempsey (R.A.S.C.) Jimmy Waite (holding the patrol's dog, Peter) and George Collis. Lieutenant Roy Fazan did not pose in this photograph and may well have been the person holding the camera.

8. Les Hawkins, former Lance Corporal in the Royal Sussex Regiment.

9. (right) Still in position the sliding cover concealing the entrance to the hideout underneath Tottington Manor. Originally a brick filled the now visible gap, made to be a hand hold for moving the cover.

10. (lower left) Beyond the entrance a passage leads down some steps into the main chamber. Above this is the present day dining room.

11. (lower right) The end of the hideout under the Tottington Manor terminates with an emergency exit tunnel (far left). This tunnel is 43 feet long and a very narrow two foot wide, the author having crawled along it to measure its length. The water tap, sticking out of the wall opposite the wash basin, is connected to the manors existing water supply and still works. Beyond the tap, in the corner of the wall, the telephone wire that connected the hideout to the lookout positioned on the Downs is still in place!

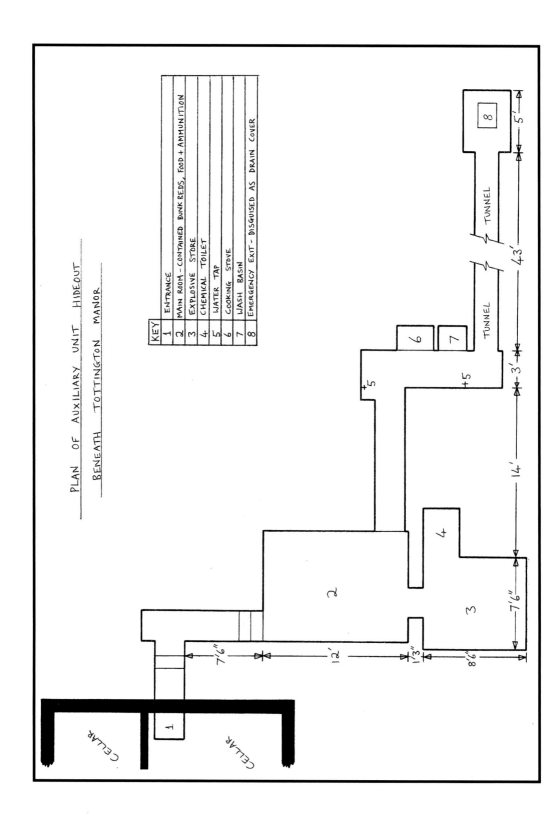

PLAN OF AUXILIARY UNIT HIDEOUT

BENEATH TOTTINGTON MANOR

KEY	
1	ENTRANCE
2	MAIN ROOM - CONTAINED BUNK BEDS, FOOD + AMMUNITION
3	EXPLOSIVE STORE
4	CHEMICAL TOILET
5	WATER TAP
6	COOKING STOVE
7	WASH BASIN
8	EMERGENCY EXIT - DISGUISED AS DRAIN COVER

PART TWO

THE SUSSEX PATROLS

4. THE HOME GUARD AUXILIARY UNITS OF SUSSEX

Sussex, which is administratively divided into East and West, kept this divide when the Auxiliary Unit patrols were formed. Patrols in the east were trained by Lieutenant Ashby and his men and those in the west by Lieutenant Fazan. In keeping with the overall secrecy of the operation, the eastern patrols knew little, if anything, about the western patrols, and vice versa.

In late 1941, when Colonel Bill Major (Colonel Gubbins' successor) had been in command of the Auxiliary Units for a year, he made a note in his personal diary about the operational state of the Auxiliary Units all around the country.

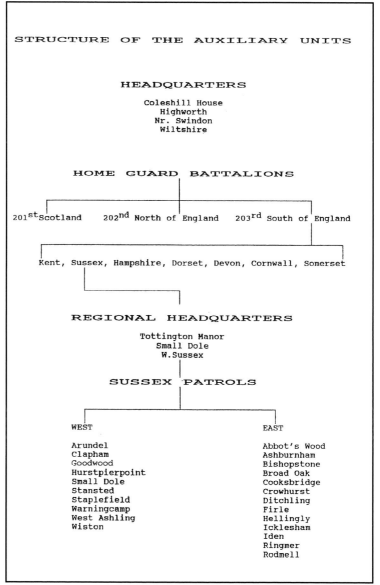

```
STRUCTURE   OF   THE   AUXILIARY   UNITS


                    HEADQUARTERS

                   Coleshill House
                      Highworth
                     Nr. Swindon
                      Wiltshire



        HOME   GUARD   BATTALIONS


201st Scotland    202nd North of England    203rd South of England


        Kent, Sussex, Hampshire, Dorset, Devon, Cornwall, Somerset



            REGIONAL   HEADQUARTERS

                  Tottington Manor
                     Small Dole
                      W.Sussex

              SUSSEX   PATROLS


        WEST                        EAST

        Arundel                     Abbot's Wood
        Clapham                     Ashburnham
        Goodwood                    Bishopstone
        Hurstpierpoint              Broad Oak
        Small Dole                  Cooksbridge
        Stansted                    Crowhurst
        Staplefield                 Ditchling
        Warningcamp                 Firle
        West Ashling                Hellingly
        Wiston                      Icklesham
                                    Iden
                                    Ringmer
                                    Rodmell
```

At that time Sussex had a total of 21 patrols, with 134 men involved. The counties bordering Sussex had far more patrols and many more members. Hampshire had 47 patrols, the greatest number in the country, with a total of 301 men. Kent had 33 patrols with a total of 208 men.

Research indicates that 23 patrols existed throughout Sussex (24 if the men at Tottington Manor are included, or even as many as 26 if the two scout patrols are taken into account, during the period of the War). The total number of men accounted for in the 23 Auxiliary Unit Patrols is 139. However, there are inevitably some gaps in the record. The actual total may have been as high as 145 men.

The smallest patrol consisted of four men and the largest eight. All were volunteers and continued to go about their daytime occupations, training usually taking place at night. Each individual patrol had excellent knowledge of its surrounding area. They only learned of the existence of neighbouring patrols through such events as inter-patrol competitions and large exercises or schemes involving the regular army.

Each patrol had an underground hideout - the Operational Base (OB). It would have been equipped as described above to support the patrol's activities in the event of an invasion. Sited near to the hideout in many cases was an Observation Post (OP) or Lookout, also of subterranean construction. Both the OB and OP were extremely well hidden, usually in woodland or thick undergrowth.

The patrol members' occupations and where they lived are correct for the years the patrols were operational. The patrols are discussed in alphabetical order for East and West Sussex respectively.

Included is a summary of extracts from Firle Patrol Leader's diary which illustrates the day to day activities of a patrol during the war. Also, a detailed description of Staplefield Patrol's hideout is given because of its excellent preservation. It is of a style typical of those built by the Royal Engineers.

EAST SUSSEX PATROLS

Abbot's Wood Patrol

The Abbot's Wood Patrol consisted of seven members. The patrol leader was Tom Dinnis who was living at Milton Court Farm near Alfriston when the patrol was formed. Later, after marrying, he became a farmer at Mays Farm near Selmeston. The other members of the patrol were: Sidney Dumbrell, a gamekeeper and rabbit catcher; John Raymond, a local farmer; Percy Robinson, a cowman; Bill Longhurst, an agricultural feed driver; Bob Wright, a local woodcutter; and John Talbot, the head gardener at Folkington Manor. Desmond Dinnis, Tom's cousin, was a member for a short time until he was called up into the RAF.

The patrol's hideout was originally intended to be in Abbot's Wood near Arlington (hence the patrol's title). However, it was discovered that the ground there was too wet, so the hideout was sited beside a chalk pit in the centre of Folkington Wood, west of Folkington Church. It was built by the Royal Engineers and measured approximately 15 feet long by 10 feet wide and was high enough to stand up in. They dug directly into the chalk and then lined the walls with wood. The roof was made of timber and covered in earth. As a finishing touch, the patrol planted small clumps of vegetation. The hideout was entered via a small trapdoor attached to a log. When the log was lifted the trapdoor came up, revealing a ladder going down into the hideout. This was its only entrance. The hideout contained plastic

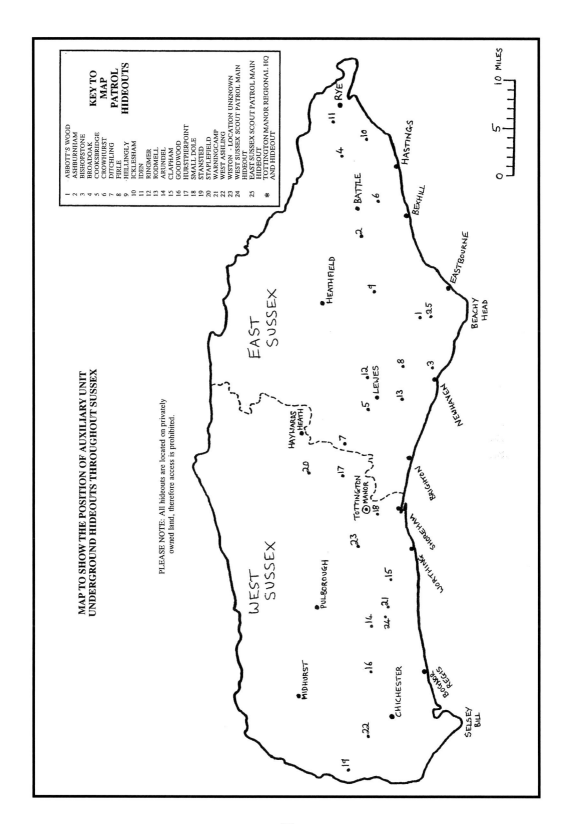

MAP TO SHOW THE POSITION OF AUXILIARY UNIT
UNDERGROUND HIDEOUTS THROUGHOUT SUSSEX

PLEASE NOTE: All hideouts are located on privately
owned land, therefore access is prohibited.

KEY TO MAP PATROL HIDEOUTS

1 ABBOTT'S WOOD
2 ASHBURNHAM
3 BISHOPSTONE
4 BROADOAK
5 COOKSBRIDGE
6 CROWHURST
7 DITCHLING
8 FIRLE
9 HELLINGLY
10 ICKLESHAM
11 IDEN
12 RINGMER
13 RODMELL
14 ARUNDEL
15 CLAPHAM
16 GOODWOOD
17 HURSTPIERPOINT
18 SMALL DOLE
19 STANSTED
20 STAPLEFIELD
21 WARNINGCAMP
22 WEST ASHLING
23 WISTON - LOCATION UNKNOWN
24 WEST SUSSEX SCOUT PATROL MAIN HIDEOUT
25 EAST SUSSEX SCOUT PATROL MAIN HIDEOUT
* TOTTINGTON MANOR REGIONAL HQ AND HIDEOUT

explosives, ammunition, food rations, a cooking stove, hurricane lamps and a water supply stored in milk churns.

Former patrol member Sidney Dumbrell remembered using the hideout regularly for training purposes. It was cramped and very uncomfortable. The patrol all did their basic training at Coleshill House. Sidney Dumbrell actually went there twice as he stood in for Tom Dinnis, who could not attend a second time due to farming commitments. The only task he performed that was different on his second visit was a night patrol around Coleshill House.

Localised training included night manoeuvres over the Downs and explosive practice at a chalk pit near Firle and in a wood at Robertsbridge. Many trips were also made to Tottington Manor.

12. **Sidney Dumbrell, former member of the Abbot's Wood Patrol.**

The patrol also had an underground lookout. This was sited about 300 yards west of the patrol's hideout. It could only accomodate one man. Sidney recalls the patrol digging the hole for the lookout by hand on a Sunday morning. The chalk they extracted from this hole was loaded onto a tractor and used on John Raymond's farm. A week after this the Royal Engineers made a trapdoor hatch and put the final touches to the lookout. Soon afterwards a telephone line was laid between the lookout and the hideout by the patrol members.

The lookout commanded a good view of the main A27 road and the Polegate to Lewes railway line. If the Germans had invaded, troop movements could have been monitored along these two routes and relayed to the hideout via the land line.

Two sites which the patrol would have tried to destroy with explosives would have been the railway line and the Sherman Bridge over the River Cuckmere on the main A27 road.

Ashburnham Patrol

The Ashburnham Patrol comprised six members. The Patrol Leader was Eric "Bunny" Wilcox who was a farm manager in Hooe. The other members were: Joe Parsons, a local farmer; Eric Johnson, who farmed Boreham Farm; Joe Norris, a farmer at Kitchenham Farm; Victor Dibben, a farmer from Hailsham; and Harold Pitcher, another local farmer. Harold Pitcher was later replaced by Ron Hart, a naval man from Hooe, who was very good with firearms. All these men were enlisted as auxiliaries by the Intelligence Officer, Captain John Gwynn, and did their basic training at Coleshill House.

The patrol's first hideout was built at the eastern end of Pannelridge Wood, north of Ashburnham. They had a lot of problems with damp and with people discovering the entrance, so the patrol decided to blow up this hideout and have another built. This second hideout was built by the Royal Engineers in Hogstye Wood about three-quarters of a mile south of the original site. It was constructed in the style of an underground Nissan hut and had an emergency exit in the form of a 50 foot long concrete tunnel. This terminated in the upper bank of a small stream. The hideout contained wooden bunk beds, food, water, ammunition and plastic explosives.

Former patrol member Eric Johnson remembered the hideout. When he was shown some photographs of the Staplefield Patrol's hideout, he thought it was very similar in size and shape to his own patrol's OB. Near to the hideout they had two small underground stores which contained extra food and ammunition. At the end of the war the hideout was emptied and blown up by the patrol.

Localised training of the patrol took place in Ashburnham Park and Battle Abbey: they quite often teamed up with the neighbouring Crowhurst Patrol. Eric Johnson recalls that his main task was to remove the rotor arms out of enemy vehicles, thus immobilising them. He also told of an attack that the Ashburnham and Crowhurst Patrols launched on the Canadian troops based in Battle Abbey. Once inside the grounds of the abbey, one of the Watter brothers, from the Crowhurst Patrol, overpowered a sentry and put on his uniform. He continued on into the abbey and promptly took the Canadian Commanding Officer prisoner. Various dummy charges were attached to vehicles and fuel supplies, making the whole attack very successful. Thinking the regular Home Guard were responsible for the attack, the Canadians visited the Chequers public house in Battle to beat them up! After this embarrassing event the Canadians reviewed and tightened up their security.

Bishopstone Patrol

The Bishopstone Patrol consisted of five members. The Patrol Leader was Lionel Willett, then owner of Bishopstone Manor Farm. The remainder of the patrol was made up of workers from Lionel Willett's farm. They were as follows: Charlie Woolmer, Jack Clark, Frank "Triggy" Turner and Fred "Chalky" White.

The patrol all did their basic training at Coleshill House. Local training was often performed in association with the neighbouring Firle Patrol. This sometimes involved army units who were stationed nearby. Charlie Woolmer remembers that the patrol would try to penetrate the army defence and place a notice on each of the guns or tanks, to simulate a plastic explosive charge, then retreat undetected. On one such night exercise, against the local Canadian army headquarters, they managed to get into the CO's office and place a small charge under his chair. The next day, when the CO came to sit down, the charge went off, causing quite a commotion within the camp.

Bill Webber and Tom Smith, from the neighbouring Firle Patrol, remembered Lionel Willet as a generous man. He would always provide food and bottles of beer for the men after training. They said that Lionel Willet had a particular fascination with the Mills bomb (more commonly known as the hand grenade). He believed this to be the ultimate weapon and carried several around with him, often strapped to his waist. He even installed a false ceiling in the outside toilet of his home, in which hand grenades could be concealed. The idea was that if he were to be arrested by the Germans, he would ask to go to the toilet and come out throwing grenades, hoping to make his escape.

On one occasion the fascination with hand grenades proved to be nearly fatal. Lionel Willett's son, John, told of the accident that happened to his father on a night exercise. The patrol was practising throwing live grenades when one failed to explode. Unexpended weapons, needless to say, had to be retrieved. Luckily, he did not have a torch with him to locate the grenade, as a few minutes after he left to get one the grenade went off.

The patrol had two rather unusual hideouts along with an underground lookout. One hideout was built out of railway sleepers and corrugated iron sheeting inside the end of the

New Barn on Lionel Willett's farm. This whole structure was covered with coal. The coal was needed as the farm had a lot of steam powered machines, so the big pile that was stored at the end of the barn did not look out of place. It contained a bunk bed for each member of the Patrol and had an emergency exit in the form of a tunnel dug under the wall of the barn leading to the surface just the other side of the wall.

The other hideout was inside a large disused water storage tank that adjoined a ruined barn on Hobb's Hawth near to Rathfinny Farm on the Downs. The tank, although narrow, was about 50 feet long and contained many bunk beds along with food, ammunition and explosives. When the lid of the tank was lifted, it looked as though the tank had been filled with rubble. However, by sliding back the trough that contained this rubble, entrance could be effected by climbing down a ladder. Approximately 200 yards to the west of this hideout was the underground lookout. This was dug into the side of the hill and only had enough room for one person. It was basically an old oil drum underneath a feeding or drinking trough. Once entrance was gained, one had to crawl along a short tunnel, then up into the oil drum. From inside, there was a commanding view of the valley down as far as Frog Firle just outside Alfriston.

Telephone lines connected the lookout to both hideouts, the two hideouts together, and the New Barn hideout to the manor house. Both the hideouts and lookout had booby traps set up in their entrances. These were made up of a pressure switch attached to an instant fuse with a detonator at the end (see Appendix). Anyone having a snoop around would have got more than they bargained for if they had tried to enter. A stranger did, in fact, set one of these off. He was found staggering around the nearby golf course, on the Downs, in a dazed condition, having nearly blown himself up.

Broad Oak Patrol

The Broad Oak Patrol consisted of six members. They were: Sidney Scott, a farmer at Glasseye Farm, Broad Oak; Len Dean, a local farm worker; the brothers Cyril and Ben Friar, both farmers at Church Farm, Brede; Harry Comport and Lionel Wray, both local farmers. It is not known which of these men was the Patrol Leader.

The patrol's hideout was sited within Moore's Wood, 500 yards to the east of Glasseye Farm, and was constructed by the Royal Engineers.

Sidney Scott's son, Robert, who still farms Glasseye Farm, remembers visiting the hideout soon after the War, only to find the main chamber had collapsed (possibly blown up by the patrol) with only the emergency exit tunnel remaining intact.

Localised training is known to have taken place at Heathfield Wood, Heathfield and Brickwall Park, Northiam. One memorable night attack took place on the Canadian soldiers based inside Brickwall Park. The park housed hundreds of troops and was a difficult target for the patrol. On successfully entering the park, the patrol laid dummy charges on various vehicles and weapons without being detected.

Cooksbridge Patrol

The Cooksbridge Patrol had seven members. Frank Martin, a farmer, was the Patrol Leader and he advised Captain John Gwynn whom to approach to form the rest of the patrol. Frank Martin was known to be quite a 'character' and seemed a natural choice of leader. The other members of the patrol were the brothers Ralph and George Cook; Jack Harmer (all local farmers); Dicky Giles, who worked in Barclays Bank in Lewes; Charley Gearing, a builder from Lewes; and Bernard Eede, a partner in the agricultural engineering business Harper and Eede in Lewes.

They all did their basic training at Coleshill House, then continued training in their own area. Localised training would take place three or four times a week. This would always be done at night to hide their activities. Training took place every Sunday; the other nights varied from week to week. Activities included mock assaults on various targets on the Downs and the surrounding countryside. The River Ouse was regularly used as an obstacle to be crossed and a local Canadian army camp was often entered and fake explosive charges set, much to the annoyance of the Canadian soldiers.

13. **Jack Harmer, former member of the Cooksbridge Patrol.**

The patrol's hideout (OB) was built by the Royal Engineers and was sited on the Downs, in part of a wood known as the Coombe Plantation, below Mount Harry, near Offham. The OB was L-shaped. The long side of the 'L' contained the bunk beds at one end, the rest of the space being devoted to food and water storage and a cooking area. Around the corner the ammunition and explosives were stored, along with the Elsan chemical toilet. The hideout's entrance was in the form of a square wooden hatch. This was attached to a branch lying on the ground, a fixed number of paces from a certain tree. When the branch was lifted it revealed a wooden ladder underneath the hatch, which went down into the hideout. This was lined with corrugated iron sheeting and had a wooden floor.

In fact, this was their second hideout, as the first one built in nearby Warningore Wood had had to be abandoned.

Jack Harmer's most vivid memory of the OB was the smell inside. This was an unusual mix of food, plastic explosives, damp earth and sweaty bodies, which after a few hours became barely tolerable. He felt an overwhelming relief on emerging through the small hatch into fresh air once again.

Close to the hideout, further up the slope of the Downs, was the patrol's lookout. This too was built by the Royal Engineers and commanded a view across the B2116 road. In the distance Frank Martin's place, Allington Farm, could be seen. The lookout was disguised as a bomb crater by scattering freshly exposed chalk around a depression directly above it. It was connected to the hideout by a direct telephone line.

They all used the hideout as part of their training but found it very uncomfortable, and it was only ever used for single night stays.

In the event of an invasion, the main aims for the patrol's sabotage activities would have been to blow up bridges, railways and any German vehicles and installations established in their area.

Ex-patrol member George Cook remembers that one morning, after they had stayed in the OB, they had a big fry up of bacon and eggs for breakfast. This was unfortunately smelled by someone passing the hideout. This person could not understand where the aroma was coming from and, being suspicious, reported it to the police. The patrol got into a lot of trouble over this incident.

Although the hideout was very well hidden, several members of the public actually found and entered the hideout during the War. The first was a young man who was out searching for badger setts at the time. He stumbled across the entrance hatch and on lifting it went inside to investigate. Looking around, and seeing the food and explosives, he decided this was obviously a highly secret place and left quickly, leaving everything as he found it. He never told anyone of his discovery until, 50 years later, he heard of the author's research into the Auxiliary Units. The second occasion was when a small boy and his friends found the hideout when the boy's dog started scratching and sniffing at the ground. On entering the hideout the boys grabbed as much of the food as they could, taking it all home with them. This prompted a lot of awkward questions from their mothers as to where it had come from.

Crowhurst Patrol

Little is known about the Crowhurst Patrol, with only three members' names coming to light. These are John Papillon and the brothers George and William Watters, all local farmers. The total number of men in this patrol is unknown, but William Watters was certainly the Patrol Leader. Their underground hideout was sited within Fore Wood, Crowhurst, to the west of the railway line that cuts the wood in half. Despite a long search of the wood, no trace of the hideout has been found.

Ditchling Patrol

The Ditchling Patrol was made up of six members. The Patrol Leader was George Thomas, a farmer from Westmeston. At the start of the War he was a first-aider who, in the event of a bombing raid, had to provide a service from Ditchling to Cuckfield. This had to be accomplished with one van and a few helpers. The service was taken over when the Air Raid Precaution Service came into being. George Thomas then joined the Home Guard and was later approached by the Auxiliary Unit's staff with a view to his becoming the Patrol

14. The emergency exit tunnel ended in the side of a bank and originally had an earth covered wooden door concealing it. With this door gone the moulded concrete recess that it fitted into can clearly be seen following the angle of the banks slope.

Leader of the Ditchling Patrol. The other patrol members were: Arthur Sharman, a coalman who was George Thomas' brother-in-law; the brothers Sam and Burt Holmes, both farmers; Harry Woods, a farm manager; and Don Atkins, another local farmer. All these men did their initial basic training at Coleshill.

The patrol's hideout was sited in the north of West Wood, adjacent to Hundred Acre Lane, in between Westmeston and Wivelsfield. It was built by the Royal Engineers using bricks, concrete, corrugated iron and wood. In form it was basically an underground Nissan hut.

The hideout was entered via an earth-covered wooden hatch. This could only be opened by pulling a release wire, which then allowed the hatch to spring up. A counter-balance weight assisted the hatch to move to a fully open position. This revealed a brick shaft going down 13 feet with a ladder made of scaffold poles set into the brickwork. At the other end of the hideout was an emergency exit in the form of a concrete tunnel 2 feet 8 inches wide and 25 feet long. This terminated in another earth covered wooden hatch that was hinged at the top. It was set at an angle of 45 degrees to emulate the slope onto which it opened out. Ventilation was provided by a network of glazed drainage pipes, four inches in diameter. These came to the surface underneath surrounding ferns and bramble bushes.

The hideout contained food, ammunition, explosives, bunk beds, a cooking stove, and a chemical toilet. Water was stored in two 30 gallon galvanised tanks. The bunk beds, when not in use, could be folded flat against the wall to create more space. A table stood in the centre of the hideout.

Former patrol member Arthur Sharman remembers they tried not to visit

15. Former Ditchling Patrol Leader George Thomas standing in front of the now exposed entrance shaft to his patrols underground hideout.

16. Arthur Sharman, former Ditchling Patrol member.

17. Burt Holmes the youngest member of the Ditchling Patrol.

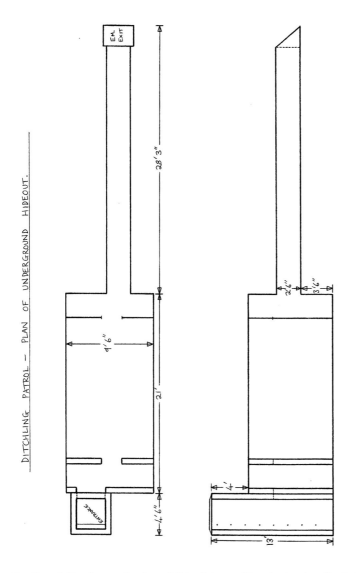

DITCHLING PATROL — PLAN OF UNDERGROUND HIDEOUT.

the hideout too often, in order to keep its whereabouts secret.

Burt Holmes recalls that localised training always took place at night and involved simulated attacks on surrounding military installations. One such attack involved the patrol having to enter a guarded radar station, either Truleigh or Poling, and laying dummy charges at the base of the aerial pylons. This they managed successfully. Another memorable attack took place on Ford Aerodrome where they had to get in and place coloured stickers on various planes to simulate attaching explosives. Some of the patrol were caught and taken to the guardroom. Once inside, the men were treated very roughly, being told to lie face down and not attempt to get up or they would be hit with a rifle butt.

Condensation was a major problem inside the hideout. George Thomas remembers having to get the Royal Engineers back and fit a false ceiling to try to alleviate the condition. He also used silica gel crystals to absorb the moisture. Because of this he used to keep a lot of the patrol's equipment in his own house. It was only a few years ago that George Thomas finally got rid of the explosives he kept there. He called in the army to assist in this task and they destroyed them harmlessly on his land. George Thomas' favourite explosive charge was a five gallon drum of petrol with a ring of Cordtex and a detonator. This combination gave, as he put it, "a spectacular explosion".

The patrol's main target, in the event of an invasion, would have been to blow up the underground fuel tanks on nearby Chailey Airfield.

After the war the hideout was emptied of its contents. Due to the shortage of building materials at the time, the corrugated iron sheeting that made up the roof of the hideout was taken out and used on George Thomas' farm.

Firle Patrol

The Firle Patrol was the smallest patrol in Sussex, having only four members. The Patrol Leader was Bill Webber, a market gardener from Firle. The other patrol members were Tom Smith, another market gardener; Jack Cornwall, a painter; and John Pilbeam, a farmhand. The latter two men both worked on the Firle Estate. All the men were originally in the Home Guard until Bill Webber was approached by Captain Gwynn with a view to his joining the Auxiliary Units and forming the Firle Patrol. They all did their basic training at Coleshill and trained locally in association with the neighbouring Bishopstone Patrol.

The patrol's hideout was sited south of the village of Firle, on the Downs, within a wood called the Firle Plantation. It was built by the Royal Engineers. The construction was of wood and galvanised steel sheeting. The whole of the inside surface was lined with cork to try and combat any condensation. The entrance hatch was opened by lifting a small tree trunk which was attached to it. The earth on top of the hatch was kept in place by netting which had moss and leaves intertwined in it to disguise its existence.

The hideout contained three bunks at one end with a stove. Food, ammunition and explosives took up most of the remaining area. Water was stored in a galvanised tank. An extension was later added to the hideout in the form of an Anderson shelter, along with an emergency exit. The chalk spoil created from this excavation was spread under the trees in the lower part of the plantation. Twenty yards north of the hideout the patrol had a small underground store which contained extra food and ammunition. To the south there was an underground lookout, connected to the hideout via a direct telephone line. It only had enough room for one man inside it, and overlooked the main trackway through the upper part of the plantation.

Patrol Leader Bill Webber and Tom Smith are the only surviving members of the patrol. They both recalled using the hideout as part of their training and many nights they walked from Firle to Bishopstone to join their neighbouring patrol in training exercises.

Due to the discovery and ransacking of the hideout by Canadian soldiers, on several occasions, in 1942, this OB was abandoned. The patrol then shared the Bishopstone OB from August, 1942.

Bill Webber recalled the time the patrol followed the River Cuckmere from its haven at Exceat all the way to Heathfield. They had to cross the river at various points during the journey. On another occasion he took a high-ranking officer, based at Coleshill, from their hideout at Firle over the Downs to Bishopstone, using only a prismatic compass and the stars to guide them.

Bill Webber's diary

Bill Webber, the Firle Patrol Leader, kept a diary of his patrol's movements during their operational years. Although the entries

18. **Bill Webber (left) and Tom Smith. The only surviving members of the Firle Patrol.**

are brief it gives a detailed account of their training, visits to Coleshill House and Tottington Manor, inter-patrol competitions and interactions with neighbouring patrols.

The diary contains 124 entries and is about 1200 words. Not every entry that appears in the diary is noted here as it would become repetitive. Only the most informative entries have been summarised, with additional details supplied by Bill Webber, who discussed the diary with the author.

The first entry was made on **5 October, 1941** and mentions a rally at Northease Manor. At this event Captain John Gwynn mapped out the autumn and winter programme for the patrols. He also gave his farewell speech on this day and introduced his successor Captain C G F Bond.

The evening of **22 October, 1941** saw the patrol practising in the Firle area. An attack was also made on the patrol's OB (Operational Base) by Badger I. Badger I was the code name for the neighbouring Bishopstone Patrol (Firle Patrol were Badger II). This exercise lasted five hours between 1800 and 2300 hours.

A combined patrol operation was held on **29 October, 1941,** with both Firle and Bishopstone Patrols at full strength. This involved an attack on a Canadian guard hut at Bishopstone. It lasted six hours between 1900 and 0130 hours. At this point it is worth remembering that all the patrol members had to do their daytime jobs as well as these night training sessions which lasted for many hours at a time.

The weekend of **8/9 November, 1941** was spent training at Tottington Manor. Lectures were given by Colonel Bill Beyts who came down from Coleshill House specifically for that weekend. Colonel Beyts was in charge of training at Coleshill.

On **29 November, 1941,** an inter-patrol competition was held at Bishopstone. Competing were members of the Bishopstone, Cooksbridge, Ringmer and Abbot's Wood Patrols. The events included Mills bomb throwing; pistol, rifle and Thompson sub-machine gun target shooting; and a night patrol efficiency test. Cooksbridge patrol came first, with 84 points; Bishopstone second, with 81 points; Abbot's Wood third, with 55 points; and Ringmer last with 43 points.

On **10 December, 1941** Firle and Bishopstone Patrols started practising map reading.

The Sussex final of the inter-patrol competitions was held at Tottington Manor, on the weekend of the **20/21 December, 1941.** This was won by Icklesham patrol, who then went on to represent Sussex in the second Home Guard patrol competition final at Coleshill House.

6 January, 1942 saw the Firle patrol engaged in an attack on tanks in Stanmer Park, just outside Brighton. This took place between 1900 and 0030 hours, the Firle Patrol being successful in their task.

On **18 January, 1942,** Bill Webber visited the Patrol's OB and found that the Canadian soldiers based at Firle Place had been digging slit trenches within the Firle Plantation. They had found the OB's entrance and forced their way in. It was not until **8 February** that he found the patrol's gallon bottle of rum was missing. On **5 March** a Court of Inquiry was held on this matter. No blame was attached to Bill Webber and a verdict was made that a person or persons unknown had taken it.

Saturday **14 March, 1942,** saw the patrol practice their drill for action, in the event of an invasion by the Germans. They had to get to their OB with all their kit. This started at 0700 hours Saturday morning and finished 1130 hours on Sunday.

On **26 March, 1942,** a Patrol Leaders' meeting was held at Allington Farm, East Chiltington. This was where the Cooksbridge Patrol Leader, Frank Martin lived. After the meeting they all visited the Cooksbridge Patrol's OB.

Captain Bond gave a lecture at Bishopstone on **15 April, 1942,** about using and concealing knives. By **23 April** this was being put into practice. The patrol attacked a sentry with the object of killing him silently with a knife. This operation lasted from 2000 to 2200 hours.

30 April, 1942 saw another Patrol Leaders' meeting at Allington Farm. The men were issued with the silenced .22 rifles, with telescopic sights, for the first time at this meeting. They were also given a new pass-word. Bill Webber could not remember what this was but recalls that such phrases as 'Rule Britannia', 'South Down' or 'Sussex Weald' were used at any given time.

It was discovered on **20 May, 1942** that the entrance to the Patrol's OB had been forced open again, and the operational rations ransacked. A Court of Inquiry was held at Bishopstone on **12 June** about the loss of the ration packs. The outcome was again that a person or persons unknown had taken them

On **25 June, 1942** a Patrol Leaders' meeting was held at Offham. They learnt that Captain Bond was leaving to take up a new appointment. They also heard details of another inter-patrol competition that was to be held on **12 July**

On the days **28 June, 2 July, 5 July and 9 July, 1942,** the patrol trained for the forthcoming competition.

The competition was held on the **12 July,** as planned, at Mary's Farm, Falmer. The Cooksbridge patrol won. Bishopstone and Firle finished third after leading. They lost valuable points on the last event called a 'relay'. This involved each man running at a target, while firing a sten gun at the same time. Out of a possible 40 points they only gained 10. This put them into third place. After the competition they were introduced to Captain Bond's replacement Captain Benson.

On **31 July, 1942,** there was a Patrol Leaders' meeting at Offham. This was the first to be chaired by Captain Benson.

31 August, 1942 saw the Firle Patrol moving their stores from their OB to the Bishopstone patrol's OB. This was because the Canadian soldiers had broken into it yet again. Thereafter Firle shared Bishopstone's OB and their own hideout was abandoned.

On **20 September, 1942,** a patrol meeting was held to work out the coming winter programme. Map reading and patrol work took place in Firle Park.

A Patrol Leaders' meeting was held at Offham on **25 September, 1942,** and the next month's programme arranged.

On **30 September, 1942** Captain Benson visited the Bishopstone Patrol. He was very impressed with the OP (lookout) and OB. While Lionel Willett showed the Captain around, the rest of the Patrol, led by Bill Webber, stalked and waylaid them.

12 October, 1942 saw both the Bishopstone and Firle patrols completing an explosives practical. Both used a standard charge (8oz of gelignite) and both charges went off successfully.

Bishopstone Patrol were visited on **29 October, 1942** by the Commander, Colonel F W R Douglas from Coleshill House. The Commander later gave an address to Patrol Leaders at Hailsham.

On **22 November, 1942,** a meeting of Patrol Leaders from all over Sussex was held at Tottington Manor. Captain Benson laid down a training programme for greater efficiency and to forestall any staleness that might be affecting the patrols.

On **1 December, 1942** the Firle Patrol had a lecture on the prismatic compass at Bishopstone. After this lecture much more map and compass work was undertaken.

The Patrol were map reading around the Chailey and Burgess Hill area on **13 December.** These were strange surroundings which made the exercise much more difficult.

The patrol practised more compass work with the Scout Patrol on **17 December, 1942,** during a night time operation in Hailsham.

On **29 December, 1942** Bill Webber and John Willett (Lionel Willet's son) attempted to cross the River Ouse in a rubber dinghy. Both men were thrown into the water when the craft suddenly turned over. They were both in full kit and the water was very cold! The exercise took place between 1830 and 2100 hours.

A weekend training course took place at Coleshill House from **8 January to 10 January, 1943.** This was the second time Bill Webber had been to Coleshill. The first time was in 1940. He was accompanied by Tom Smith, Jack Clark and Charlie Woolmer. Tom Smith and Bill Webber took part in a night operation around Coleshill House. Bill Webber attained full marks for Mills bomb throwing, one of his favourite events.

The weekend **16/17 January, 1943** saw a Patrol Leaders' course at Tottington Manor. This was a very intensive course which included such items as the right and wrong way to stalk, behaviour in the OB, firing of the sten gun, revolver and rifle, lectures on the course of the War, first-aid, care of arms, and giving orders.

On **31 January, 1943,** the Firle Patrol visited the Rodmell Patrol to see their OB and OP.

11 February, 1943 saw the patrol crossing the River Ouse at Durham Farm, near Tarring Neville, and walking down to Brookside Farm just outside of Piddinghoe. They returned the same way. The patrol used a rubber dinghy, and both river crossings were successful. This exercise took place between 1900 and 2300 hours.

On **16 February, 1943** there was a Patrol Leaders' meeting at Allington Farm with Captain Benson as chairman. They all heard that Lieutenant Ashby and the Scouts were leaving the Auxiliary Units to return to their regiments. The reason given for this was that they had to prepare and be available for the Normandy landings.

Soon after this the Auxiliary Units were asked for volunteers to be parachuted into France as a pre-invasion plan. This would entail two weeks of intensive parachute training which the Auxiliary Units lacked. Both Bill Webber and Tom Smith volunteered from the Firle Patrol.

Entries in the diary are few and far between after this date. This was due to the threat of German invasion passing and training becoming more relaxed. Even so the Firle Patrol continued to train as a patrol until the stand down was ordered on **18 November, 1944.** The last entry in the diary is **9 January, 1944** and mentions a patrol course at Tottington Manor.

Hellingly Patrol

The Hellingly patrol consisted of seven members. The Patrol Leader was John Richards, the farm manager at Park Farm, Hellingly, which was associated with Hellingly Hospital. The other members were good friends of John Richards who he knew he could trust. They were Burt Harris, a farmer from Fontmills, north of the Hellingly Parish; Jock

Venus, a market gardener from Herstmonceux; Reginald Comford, an agricultural contractor from Horsebridge; John White, a peach grower, also from Horsebridge; Jack Baker, a gamekeeper; and Dougie Land, a farm worker. The latter two men both lived in Chiddingly. All these men referred to John Richards as 'Guv'. They each had a number to identify themselves while on patrol. This greatly simplified communications. The patrol all went to Coleshill for their basic training.

Their hideout was sited within the eastern half of Park Wood, Hellingly. It was built by the Royal Engineers and constructed of corrugated iron and timber. An emergency exit was added later by the patrol in the form of a corrugated iron tunnel which led out into the bank of a small stream. They dug this by hand, backfilling the spoil over the tunnel, levelling it off, then covering the soil with undergrowth.

The hideout was regularly used for training purposes. The patrol often stayed inside from Friday night through to Sunday evening. They always took enough food and water so as not to use any of their issued rations. A small underground lookout in the form of an Anderson shelter was positioned near to the hideout. They were connected by a direct telephone line.

Former Patrol Leader John Richards recalled some of his patrol's localised training. One attempted mock attack was on the radar station at Beachy Head, near Eastbourne. The patrol set out from Alfriston, in complete darkness, making its way over the Downs towards the radar station. On arriving at the site they discovered it was surrounded by a ring of broken china. This would have made a silent approach to the objective impossible, and an attempt to enter here would have alerted the sentries to their presence. This impassable barrier meant the only possible way into the station was via the main road, which was of course guarded. Two members of the patrol tried to get into the back of a lorry which was just about to enter the radar station. They had to abandon this idea when someone decided to get out of the lorry as they were about to climb in.

A more successful mock attack took place on the Canadian troops stationed in Heathfield Park, Heathfield. The captain in charge of the scheme promised to give them a bottle of whiskey if the patrol was successful. The weather was against them as it had been raining all evening and continued to rain as the patrol prepared for their attack. They entered the park with blackened faces.

While the rest of the patrol were marking vehicles and guns, to simulate explosive charges being laid, John Richards and another patrol member went off in another direction. He decided to mingle in with some despatch riders who were standing around smoking. John Richards lit up a cigarette too, and after a while they made their way to the officers mess. He calmly entered the mess, with a revolver in one hand and a hand grenade in the other, announcing "gentlemen, you

19. John Richards, former patrol leader of the Hellingly Patrol.

are all dead".

On explaining who he and his companion were, along with the purpose of their attack, the two men were congratulated by the officers and each given a drink of whisky. They then both left the park the way they had entered. Security around the park was stepped up after this incident.

In the event of an invasion, the patrol had various trees targeted for felling, in order to block roads. The railway line would have been blown up north of Hellingly station.

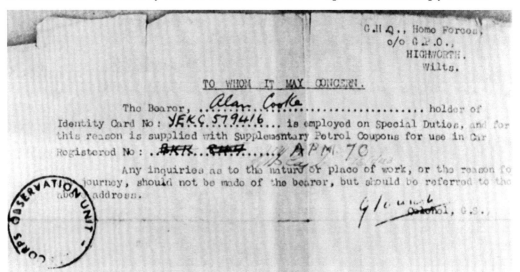

20. Alan Cookes pass explaining why he is supplied with extra petrol coupons. Note the address in the event of any queries is c/o G.P.O. HIGHWORTH, WILT. rather than Coleshill House. The pass is signed by Colonel Glenusk, the man in charge at Coleshill at the time of issue. Because Mr Cooke changed his car the pass had to be amended and counter signed by the intelligence officer Captain Benson in 1943.

Icklesham Patrol

The Icklesham Patrol was made up of six members. Jack Merrick, a local farmer, was the Patrol Leader. The other members were Dick Merrick, Jack's brother; Alan Cooke; Colin Cooke; Don Cooke; and Jack Jones, local farmers. They were all originally members of the regular Home Guard before being approached about joining the auxiliary units. They attended Coleshill House for their basic training. The area their patrol covered was from Udimore down to Hastings and back along to Winchelsea.

The patrol's hideout was situated close to a sand pit within Guestling Wood, near Icklesham. This was built by the Royal Engineers as the patrol did not have time to construct it due to farming commitments. It was built of timber and corrugated iron and measured approximately 15 feet long by 10 feet wide and was high enough to stand up in. Entrance was gained by lifting a counterbalanced hatch concealed by twigs and leaves and then climbing down a wooden ladder. An emergency exit tunnel, made from timber, ran out from the hideout for about 15 feet to the edge of the sandpit. The hideout contained bunk beds, food, ammunition, explosives, water (stored in milk churns), a cooking stove and a chemical toilet. The bunk beds were stacked three high to save space, the lowest one being just off the ground.

Former patrol member Colin Cooke remembers staying inside the hideout many times as part of their training. The bunks were functional but uncomfortable. He also recalled many visits to Tottington Manor for training and going to a place called Huntley, near Aberdeen, in Scotland for three days training. This involved flying over an area to give the men idea of the terrain, then landing and performing exercises within the area, drawing on the knowlege they had gained from the aerial view. One such exercise involved targets suddenly springing up within a wood which had to be shot at with a sten gun whilst on the move.

Iden Patrol

The Iden Patrol was the most easterly Patrol in East Sussex, and its area lay approximately 75 miles from Tottington Manor.

The Patrol had six members when it was first formed. However, after a year, one of its members (Frank Reeve, a farmer at Lea Farm, Iden) was called up into the army and was not replaced. The Patrol Leader was John Winter, a farmer at Saltbarn Farm, Playden. The other members of the Patrol were Jack Matthews, a farmer at Leasam Farm, Iden; Jack Goodwin, the owner of an agricultural engineering firm in Rye; Walter Dawes, a farm worker; and Bill Bailey, a commercial artist who worked for newspapers and also undertook Royal commissions. He lived nearby in Beckley.

They all went to Coleshill for their basic training. Localised training took place three or four times a week and mainly involved the patrol practising with various explosives on tree stumps and disused rabbit warrens.

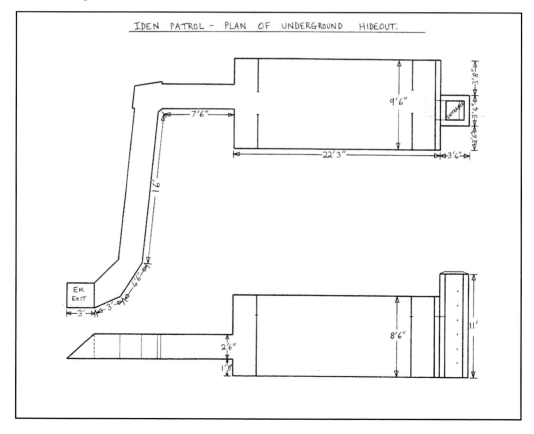

21. Looking down the 11 feet deep entrance shaft to the Iden patrol hideout. Only half a rung of the ladder remains in place. The recess in the concrete at the top would have allowed its earth covered wooden hatch to locate and sit down in place.

22. Some original shelving still in place in one of the hideouts 2'6" wide storage areas.

23. The emergency exit tunnel terminates in the bank of a small stream. Like the Ditchling patrol hideout it would have had a flush fitting earth covered wooden door and would only have been used if really necessary.

The patrol's hideout was sited in Norland Wood, 500 yards east of Peasmarsh Church. It was built by the Royal Engineers. Construction would have been difficult as it was positioned near the bottom of a steep slope, next to a stream. The problem of transporting materials to the site must have been formidable, let alone the actual building work. The hideout had a similar design to the Ditchling and Staplefield Patrol's OBs and was basically an underground Nissan hut.

Entrance was gained by pulling a concealed cable release. This let an earth-covered wooden hatch lift up slightly, so someone could get their fingers underneath it. The hatch had about four inches of soil on top of it, and a counterbalance weight was required to assist in lifting it. Once opened a brick built shaft with a ladder led down into the hideout.

At the other end of the hideout was an emergency exit in the form of a two foot eight inch concrete tunnel. It was thirty feet in length and terminated in the bank of the stream. This too had an earth-covered wooden hatch but had no cable release. If used it would have been pushed open from the inside. The hideout contained bunk beds, ammunition, explosives, food, water, a cooking stove and an Elsan chemical toilet.

The patrol visited the hideout every weekend but, unlike other patrols, they never stayed overnight as part of their training.

Former patrol member, Jack Matthews, recalled some of the targets the patrol would have attempted to sabotage in the event of an invasion. These included the railway line at Rye and the two main roads running out of Rye to Ashford and Folkstone. He also remembered their patrol, along with several adjacent patrols, going to a meeting at Catsfield. There a high ranking officer explained how volunteers were needed to be parachuted into France as part of a pre-invasion plan for the Normandy Landings. All the men put their names forward.

Ringmer Patrol

This patrol was made up of eight members. The Patrol Leader was Ralph Edmondson, a farmer who lived at Clayhill House, Ringmer. The other members were Matthew Craig, a farmer at Goat Farm, Ringmer; Henry Piper, a shepherd/farm hand who lived near Glyndebourne; Stuart Andrews, a farmer at Upper Clayhill Farm, Ringmer; Thomas Veness, who worked as a woodcutter in the saw mills within Plashett Wood and lived close to the mills; Percy Smith, the then landlord of the Cock Inn; Gerald Wibbley, a professor in agriculture; and Dick Muddle who worked as a mechanic at the Ashtree garage. This garage was owned by local man Jack Goldsmith. However, at the start of the War he was called up into the RAF and the garage was taken over and run by the wartime Ministry of Agriculture; this explains Gerald Wibbley's involvement, as he worked for the ministry. Both the garage and inn were on the A26 Ringmer to Uckfield road. The men all did their basic training at Coleshill.

The patrol's hideout was sited 400 yards east of Clayhill House on Ralph Edmondson's land. It was built by the Royal Engineers into an existing mound called a 'Motte', thought to be an ancient site of a castle or camp. Today the site is a protected ancient monument! Two hundred yards to the south-west the patrol had a small underground store for extra food and ammunition, near the present day triangulation point.

All the patrol members have now passed away but Beatrice Veness remembers some of the training her husband and the rest of the patrol did during the War. The patrol would stay in the hideout overnight as part of their training. On one occasion this nearly ended in tragedy. The patrol members were all inside the hideout when, after a while, everyone

24. The Ringmer Patrol. Taken towards the end of the war, this is the only photograph of a Sussex patrol in uniform known to have been taken. Back row from left to right:- Matthew Craig, Tom Veness, Gerald Wibbley, Stuart Andrews and Henry Piper. Front row from left to right:- Dick Muddle, Ralph Edmundson (patrol leader) and Percy Smith.

became drowsy. No one had opened the air vents and they were all slowly suffocating. Local training took place in Plashett Park, a favourite exercise being to cross any of its three lakes via a rope strung across it. Whilst a patrol member was making his way across the rest of the patrol would be throwing thunderflashes under him.

In the early months of the patrol's formation, around the time of the expected invasion, they had an exercise which involved taking part of a gun from a gun emplacement at Seaford. The patrol got away with an important piece of the gun whilst the gun operators were fast asleep. After it was found how this item of equipment had been removed the gunners were severely reprimanded for being asleep on duty.

The patrol also made a night attack on a hall full of Canadian soldiers in Brighton. Tom Veness played a major role in the operation. To get to the hall he had to go through someone's house. He knocked on the front door and a woman answered it. She watched in disbelief as he ran through her house and out of the back door, then climbed the brick wall at the bottom of her garden. He then proceeded to get onto the roof of the hall, where he removed a couple of slates, and threw in thunderflashes among the troops in the hall, causing total confusion.

Beatrice Veness has supplied a photograph of the Ringmer Patrol in uniform. This was professionally taken in a studio in Lewes High Street. She recalled that Stuart Andrews was late for the sitting and ended up changing into his uniform out in the street.

Rodmell Patrol

This patrol was formed in May 1940. The area they covered was from Newhaven to Lewes, the River Ouse being their eastern boundary. The Lewes to Falmer railway line marked their northern boundary and the western limit was defined by the B2132 road from Falmer to Rottingdean. The cliffs between Rottingdean along the coast to Newhaven formed a natural boundary to the south.

The first Patrol Leader was Guy Woodman. He remained Patrol Leader until September 1940. Guy Woodman was a local farmer but had to relinquish his leadership when he moved out of the area. An existing patrol member, Frank Dean, took over as Patrol Leader when Guy Woodman left. He was a blacksmith at Rodmell, and remained the patrol's leader for rest of its operational years. The patrol was composed of seven members at any one time. These members were as follows: Wilfred Beagly; Lesley Coustick; Cliff Pettit; Algernon Potter, all local farmers; Harry Gregory, a gardener; and Tom Carr, a farmer from Kingston near Lewes.

They were all originally members of the regular Home Guard and after the patrol was formed they continued to train alongside them for a while. After doing their basic training at Coleshill House they ceased training with the regular Home Guard and trained together as an auxiliary patrol.

This localised training took place two to three times a week and consisted of mock attacks, sometimes on tanks based at Stanmer Park near Falmer. River crossings, night time manoeuvres on the Downs and combined exercises with the army were also used in the training schedule. Sometimes the patrol would go to Tottington Manor to use the assault course that was set up in its grounds.

The patrol's underground hideout, known to them as the OB, was sited on the Downs, near a place called Breaky Bottom about one and a half miles east of Rodmell village. The patrol dug the hole into the chalk for the hideout but the Royal Engineers actually built the interior and the roof. It was lined with corrugated iron and wood. The hideout measured 20 feet long, 12 feet wide and about 9 feet high. At one end it had a square hatch for an

25. Frank Dean, former Rodmell patrol leader.

26. Tom Carr, former member of the Rodmell patrol and the first ex member of the auxiliary units in Sussex that the author managed to locate when starting his research.

entrance and another one at the other end for an emergency exit. These both had wooden ladders underneath them. The hatches were both covered with about four inches of soil with vegetation growing in it (stinging nettles, grass etc). Ventilation was provided by approximately four two and half inch wide pipes leading to the surface. The roof/ceiling was made up of 9 inch by 4 inch timbers.

The hideout contained bunk beds, a water tank, food, a cooking stove, ammunition, plastic explosives, a gallon bottle of rum and an Elsan chemical toilet. The water tanks always had water in them and purification tablets were supplied to make it drinkable. Inside the hideout it was constantly damp and to try to combat this Frank Dean devised a box, about six inches square, filled with silica gel to absorb the moisture out of the air. He suspended this from the ceiling and placed a barrel underneath to catch the excess water that dripped down from it. Frank Dean can remember this barrel would fill at a fast rate and would have to be regularly emptied.

During the War the army carried out a lot of training and target practice on the Downs. On one occasion an army vehicle pulling a gun behind it stopped on top of the Rodmell Patrol's hideout. The roof was strong enough to take the weight but the entrance hatch gave way and one of the gun wheels became stuck. This naturally revealed the existence of the hideout to the soldiers, who after removing the wheel, entered the hideout and stole the patrol's rum ration. When Frank Dean found the entrance broken, and the rum missing, he reported it to his superiors. This led to an enquiry to ascertain who had taken the rum. The enquiry concluded that the rum was taken by a person or persons unknown.

In 1945 Frank Dean removed the timbers that made up the roof of the hideout. The timbers were used on various building projects around Rodmell village.

After the War Frank Dean and the other patrol members were given the special lapel badge to commemorate being part of the Auxiliary Units. This was presented to them at a dinner party in Brighton.

At the time of writing Frank Dean continues to work at his forge in Rodmell.

WEST SUSSEX PATROLS

Arundel Patrol

The Arundel Patrol consisted of seven members. The Patrol Leader was Frank Penfold, owner of an agricultural engineering firm, who lived in Walberton to the west of Arundel. Frank Penfold began his Auxiliary Unit career as a member of Leslie Drewett's Goodwood Patrol. However, this was only for a few months until he was asked to form the Arundel Patrol.

The other members of the patrol were George Cross, who worked for the Forestry Commission; David Blackwood, a farm foreman at Walberton; George Birch, who worked for Frank Penfold as a blacksmith and welder; Jim Lee, a farmer at Burton Mill Farm, South Stoke; and a man called Philips who worked for the Ministry of Supply. All the men did their basic training over one weekend at Coleshill.

Localised training took place in the surrounding area with live grenade practice in Blakehurst chalk pit, and what the patrol termed "thuggery" was practised on Long Down near to Goodwood Patrol's hideout. Often training involved neighbouring patrols. One combined mock attack took place on the radar station at nearby Poling.

The patrol's hideout was sited in the north of Houghton Forest and contained bunk beds, water, food, ammunition and two metal dustbins full of explosives of various sorts. An emergency exit tunnel about 50 feet long ran out from the hideout. Some fifty yards to the south was a small underground lookout, connected to the hideout via a direct telephone line.

Former patrol leader Frank Penfold described the various weapons which his patrol acquired during its operational years. They had two Colt automatic pistols: a .35 and the larger .45. Frank recalled the .22 silenced rifle which they were told was for sniping at German commanders. In his opinion it would have been better used on any tracker dogs sent to find the men. After the patrol was stood down, Frank kept several items of equipment, though he now has only his fighting knife, the 'Fairbairn Dagger'. When the men of Arundel Patrol were issued with these knives, they found the handles too narrow, so wound them round with plastic tape to build up the grip to the desired thickness.

Clapham Patrol

It is uncertain how many members this patrol had, but of the many names that have been suggested, the following five men were definitely involved: Joe Avery, a local gardener; his brother Clem Avery, a plumber by trade, but at that time working for the Forestry Commission; Alec Kennel, a local gamekeeper; 'Bunny' Booker, a woodcutter; and Charley Brooker, the foreman at Clapham brickworks. Ronald Jordan, who also worked at Clapham brickworks, is thought to have been a member: he could have become involved through his association with Charley Brooker. However, this is unconfirmed. It is not known which man was the Patrol Leader.

The patrol's hideout and an underground store were sited within Clapham Wood. The hideout was built into the side of a chalk pit and contained three separate rooms, the largest measuring approximately 12 feet by 9 feet. It had an emergency exit tunnel running out into the inside face of a kiln in the chalk pit. An underground lookout was sited about 500 yards to the north of the hideout, within a hedgerow.

Les Hawkins of the West Sussex Scout Patrol remembers helping to build both the hideout and lookout. During the hideout construction, some local people wandered too close for comfort, prompting Lieutenant Fazan to lay many booby traps in an attempt to deter this, while giving his men advance warning that someone was approaching. The booby traps were made up of a small amount of explosive attached to a pull switch, with a trip wire to set it off. Lieutenant Fazan was assembling one of these traps when it accidentally went off, peppering his face and chest with soil. He spent the next two weeks recovering in Worthing Hospital.

The only known localised training took place at Goring Castle, south of Clapham Wood. This was home to a large number of Canadian soldiers, and had a perimeter fence of barbed wire. One night-time attack by the patrol on the castle could have ended in disaster had they been caught, since nobody had forewarned the Canadians guarding it not to fire live ammunition if they encountered intruders.

Goodwood Patrol

The Goodwood Patrol had seven members. The Patrol Leader was Lesley Drewett, a farmer at Colworth Farm, Colworth, between Chichester and Bognor Regis. The other members were Charley Longlands, a farmhand on Lesley Drewett's farm; Bunny Bailey, a farmer at Elbridge Farm, Colworth; Jack Code, a farmer at Courthill Farm, Slindon; Reginald Heaver, a farmer from Oving, and his brother Alan who lived at Fishbourne and whose occupation involved extracting, processing and marketing sand and gravel; and a Mr Bingham, a coalman from Bognor. All the men did their basic training at Coleshill.

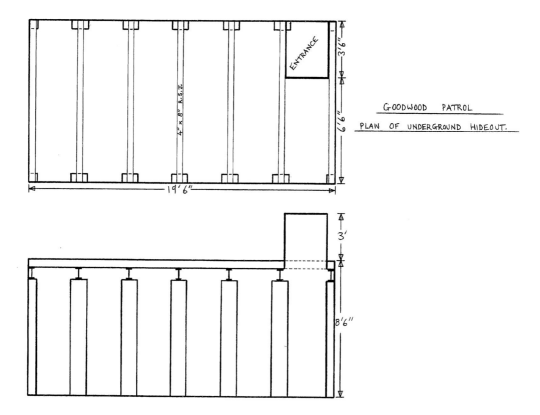

GOODWOOD PATROL

PLAN OF UNDERGROUND HIDEOUT.

27. Inside the only chamber of the Goodwood hideout. Note the R.S.J. beams supporting the roof and the smooth well-built concrete walls. No other patrols hideout in Sussex has been built to these standards.

The patrol's hideout was a single underground chamber measuring 19 feet 6 inches long, 10 feet wide and 8 feet 6 inches high, situated in a woodland area called 'The Thicket', three quarters of a mile to the west of Eartham.

Built by the Royal Engineers, its walls and floor are constructed of solid concrete with the 6 inch thick reinforced concrete ceiling supported by five evenly-spaced 8 inch by 4 inch RSJ beams. This overly-solid construction, coupled with the absence of an emergency exit, is unusual for an Auxiliary Unit hideout in Sussex. Entrance into the hideout was gained by lifting an old tree stump which was attached to a hinged trapdoor. This revealed a wooden ladder going down into the hideout. Inside were four bunk beds, ammunition, explosives, a large food store, and water stored in two galvanised tanks. Two hundred yards to the north east of the hideout was the patrol's OP. This was basically a 6 feet by 4 feet trench with a camouflaged top over it. One man would have been housed inside, relaying any details back to the hideout via a direct telephone line.

Former patrol member Alan Heaver remembered doing a great deal of training with the neighbouring West Ashling patrol of which his other brother, Jack, was a member. On one such night-time training exercise, the two patrols had to simulate laying an explosive charge on a guarded anti-aircraft gun at a place called Temple Bar about one mile north of Tangmere airfield. The guards around the 'Ack-Ack' gun had been warned that an attack would be attempted some time that night, and not to fire live ammunition at the attackers. The two patrols met up at Shopwyke, about two miles away from the target site. Alan Heaver was teamed up with Stanley Mason, the West Ashling patrol leader.

As they made their way towards Temple Bar Alan Heaver, being the younger man, started to pull away from Stanley Mason and reached the target site first. He entered the perimeter of the site, got right up to the gun, chalked a swastika on it and escaped the same way without detection. He had completed the exercise long before the other men arrived. Unsure what to do with the remaining time, he decided to have another go and chalk a second swastika on the gun. This was a bad move: he was caught, as were all the others eventually.

28. Alan Heaver former Goodwood Patrol member.

All the men were taken to see an army officer (identity unknown) at Halnaker Wind-mill. The officer consoled the men on their failed attack, at which Alan Heaver said he had managed to mark the gun and was only caught on his second attempt. The officer, most put out, demanded to be shown the swastika and drove Alan Heaver back to the site to see for himself.

Hurstpierpoint Patrol

The Hurstpierpoint Patrol had six members. The Patrol Leader was Percy Tulley, the son of Walter Tulley, founder of Master and Tulley, a general store in Hurstpierpoint selling everything from groceries and clothes to furnishings. The other patrol members were Bill Baron, a market gardener at the local Gears nursery; Ernest 'Jimmy' Williams, a baker in Hurstpierpoint High Street; Wally Crook, a farmer, and the brothers 'Pop' and Basil Stringer, both builders. 'Pop' Stringer, as he was known to everyone, was later called up

29. The three foot square entrance shaft to the Hurstpierpoint Patrol hideout is the only evidence of its existence. The main chamber having collapsed many years ago.

into the regular army, but it is not known whether the patrol took on another member to replace him.

The patrol's underground hideout was sited in a small wood to the north of Wolstonbury Hill, just on the edge of the Downs. It was built by the Royal Engineers who constructed it out of timber and corrugated iron sheeting. It is unknown whether the patrol had an underground lookout.

Part of the patrol's training included mock attacks on Danny House which is reputed to have 365 rooms within it.

Jimmy Williams' brother Frank recalled that Jimmy had, through the excellent training he received, become expert in explosives: he knew even more than Frank's associates in the regular army. Jimmy never did reveal to his brother the whereabouts of the patrol's hideout but, much to Frank's delight, the author was able to tell him its exact location.

Small Dole Patrol

The Small Dole Patrol had eight members. The Patrol Leader was George Cooper who worked for a company called Jenner and Higgs as a corn merchant, which meant he had a petrol allowance. He lived in Small Dole. George Cooper was a veteran of the First World War, when he was a bomber pilot in the Royal Flying Corps. The methods used in those days were very primitive, the bombs being lobbed out of the plane by hand! The other patrol members were Richard Griffiths, another World War I veteran, who was a farmer at Merrion Farm to the north of Ashurst; the brothers George and Fred Cooke, both farmers from Woodmancote; Bernard Chaplin, a local gunsmith; Bernard Coleman, a farmer from Henfield; William Parker, a farmer at Little Bently Farm, Henfield and Ralph Paine, occupation unknown. All the men did their basic training at Coleshill House.

Localised training included one memorable mock attack on Shoreham Airport. After the war, George Cooper would tell his friends about the time he and his patrol entered the airport at night time by getting under the barbed wire perimeter fence and proceeding to lay various fake charges on the runway and planes, leaving the same way as they got in without being detected by the army who were guarding the whole area.

The patrol's hideout was sited in a small wood beside the A283 Steyning to Shoreham road, 300 yards to the north of Old Erringham Farm, Old Shoreham, and was built by the Royal Engineers. It is not known if there was an underground lookout.

George Cooper kept extra supplies of ammunition and explosives buried in his back garden. These remained buried until after his death some twenty years ago, and were only discovered when the new owners of his house were carrying out alterations to the garden: they unearthed the secret cache, which not only gave them a fright but gave the authorities the problem of how to remove it all and make the area safe.

30. The Small Dole Patrol got together for a reunion of all the West Sussex Patrols on the 12th December 1946. This was the menu issued to all the former patrol members. The top section is 'lifted' from the cover of the 'Countrymans Diary' training manual. At the bottom it jokingly describes the hideouts throughout West Sussex as if up for sale.

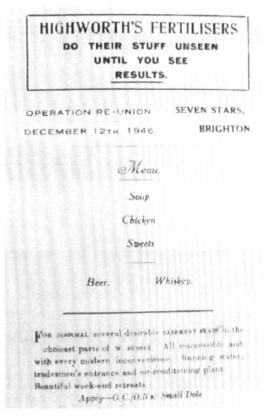

Staplefield Patrol

The Staplefield Patrol consisted of seven members. Unfortunately, only four members names are known. The Patrol Leader was Frank Baker, a farmer at Home Farm, Staplefield, who later went on to become the Mayor of Brighton. The other members were close friends and associates of his. They were Cecil Mills, a gamekeeper and baliff, who lived in Handcross; Les Moore, a milkman from Handcross; and Gerald Cummings, a cattle farmer in Bolney.

Nora Mills, wife of ex-patrol member Cecil Mills, recalled how her husband had kept his involvement in the Auxiliary Units secret while the patrol was operational. She knew he was training with explosives, but thought he was part of the regular Home Guard. After the War he explained what he had been doing.

The patrol's hideout was sited in Foxashes Wood, between Ansty and Bolney, near to the A272 road. It was built by local Canadian soldiers. They were used because it was known that they would be moving to another area after finishing the hideout, taking knowledge of its whereabouts with them, thus helping the site to remain secret.

Frank Baker's youngest son David showed the author the exact location of the hideout. On entering the structure it soon became apparent that this was the best preserved

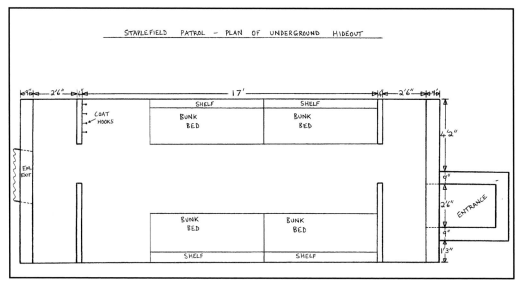

example in Sussex, with the original bunk beds, shelving, a table and even coat hooks still in place.

The hideout was constructed on a solid concrete base with one foot six inches high brick built sidewalls. These low brick walls support the corrugated iron that is arched across to form the roof of the hideout. The only entrance to the hideout was beneath an earth covered wooden hatch. When lifted this revealed a brick built shaft with a ladder made up of scaffold poles set into the brickwork. Beyond this two internal walls, both with locking doors, separate the main chamber of the hideout from the entrance shaft, at the eastern end, and the 75 feet long emergency exit tunnel at the western end. The main chamber contained the bunk beds and storage space for essential equipment along with an ingeniously designed drop-leaf table. One leg sat on the concrete floor while the other leg was made to be about a foot longer and supported the whole table by locating in a purpose-built socket in the floor. The three feet wide emergency exit tunnel ran out into the bank of a nearby pond. Its end also being concealed by an earth covered wooden hatch. Ventilation was provided by a network of four inch diameter glazed drainage pipes that came to the surface within the surrounding undergrowth.

Although the hideout was built by Canadian soldiers it was the job of the men in the West Sussex Scout Patrol to camouflage its existence. Former member Sidney Gaston recalls back-filling soil over the the hideout, taking great care to conceal the air vents. Some of these had clay moulded around the end of the pipes to make them look like rabbit holes. The men placed rabbit droppings around the holes for extra effect. As a finishing touch small trees, bushes and general undergrowth was replanted over the top of the hideout.

In November 1994 the Staplefield Patrol's hideout reached celebrity status when it was seen by millions of viewers on 'Schofields Quest' as part of the author's appeal for information concerning the Auxiliary Units in Sussex.

31. The Staplefield Patrol hideout in surprisingly good condition after all these years, with half the bunk beds still standing and a door still in place. Note the lock and coat hook on the door. Beyond the doorway is the entrance shaft.

32. Looking in the opposite direction the start of the 3 feet wide, 75 feet long emergency exit tunnel can be seen through the doorway. Note more coat hooks still in place on the wall. With the door and its frame now gone this doorway shows a fault in its design, a lintel was not put above the frame to support the brickwork.

33. Shelves were positioned beside the bunk beds to maximise the use of space within the hideout.

34. Junction of the glazed ventilation pipes in the centre of the roof. These provided ventilation via convection currents and natural air movement from the wind.

Stansted Patrol

The Stansted Patrol was the most westerly sited unit in West Sussex and consisted of six members. The Patrol Leader was Bill Wolfries, the head keeper for Stansted Forest. The other members were George Huxham, a farmer at Pitlands Farm, Up Marden; Ronald Peel, a farmer at Lodge Farm, Forest Side; Jim Rousell, a driver from the Rowlands Castle area; and Mr Butler a gamekeeper from the Lordington Estate. All patrol members went to Coleshill for their basic training. Localised training often took place within Stansted Forest. This included firing practice with the patrol's various guns and learning how to make up explosive charges, often joining three together over a given distance so that they would all detonate at the same time.

The patrol's hideout was sited in the side of a chalk pit in the north-eastern end of Stansted Forest. It was built of wood and corrugated iron with one small entrance hatch and an emergency exit tunnel which ran out to the bottom face of the chalk pit. About 400 yards to the west of the hideout, the patrol had a small underground lookout. Both were connected by a direct telephone line and constructed by the Royal Engineers. The lookout commanded a good view of the main Stansted road.

Former patrol members Ron Peel and George Huxham recalled using the hideout regularly for overnight stays, and the many visits to Tottington Manor as part of their training. Ron Peel also remembered going to Coleshill and having to set fake charges on a plane as part of his basic training.

The only other patrols with which they can remember training were the West Ashling and Warningcamp patrols.

35. Stansted Patrols only surviving members Ronald Peel (left) and George Huxham.

36. View showing the construction of the Stansted Patrol hideout, note the combination of worked and unworked timber along with the corrugated iron. The wires leading up into a glazed pipe would have connected the Patrol's lookout to the hideout via battery operated telephones.

Warningcamp Patrol

The Warningcamp Patrol had five members. Its Patrol Leader was Jack Lock, a farmer at Blakehurst Farm, Warningcamp. The other members were Ted Cooper, a farmer at Seldon Farm near Patching; Reginald Pitts, a farmer at North Stoke Farm; Harry Hayler, a local gamekeeper and his son Douglas Hayler who worked for the River Board.

The patrol's hideout was sited within Wepham Wood, nearly a mile to the north-east of Blakehurst Farm, and constructed at night-time by Canadian Engineers. A farmhand who worked for Jack Lock was mystified when he arrived early for work to find the tractor's engine was still warm, although it appeared not to have moved from where he had parked it the night before. Unknown to him, the Canadian Engineers had been using it all night for transporting their equipment and materials to the construction site of the hideout.

In the event of an invasion the patrol's main targets were the railway and river bridges at Arundel, along with the A284 road to Littlehampton. It is thought that the Ford Airfield was also a target area.

Jack Lock's eldest son Michael recalled that his father's patrol was approached for volunteers to be parachuted into France as a pre-invasion plan for the Normandy landings. The men were to receive two weeks' training, probably at Coleshill, involving an intensive course which would include actual jumps out of a Lysander aircraft.

Not only the Sussex patrols were approached: Auxiliary Unit patrols all around the country were asked for volunteers. Even though a great many members volunteered, the plan, for some unknown reason, was never put into action. A popular theory is that it was heavily opposed by the Pensions Department due to the fact that all the men were volunteers and, if they were killed over in France, a lot of claims could be made by their wives and families.

The plan was not really practical, as it went against the very reason for the men being chosen for the Auxiliary Units in the first place: they had to have excellent knowledge of their local area to be able to move around in the dark. Placing these men in unknown French countryside would have been ineffective and possibly disastrous.

West Ashling Patrol

The West Ashling patrol had six members. The Patrol Leader was Stanley Mason, a large man known as 'Jumbo' to his friends, who was a farmer at West Stoke Farm, West Ashling. The other patrol members were Charles Goodyear, a local agricultural engineer; Arthur Goodyear (no relation), a farmer in West Ashling; Jack Heaver, a farmer in Funtington, whose brothers Reg and Alan were in the Goodwood Patrol; Dick Hadland, a farm worker on Downs Farm, Funtington; and Cecil Butler, another farmer in West Ashling.

All the men did their initial training at Coleshill and continued with localised training, usually under the cover of darkness but sometimes on a Sunday morning: this would generally involve playing football! The patrol regularly used its hideout for training purposes, pretending that the invasion had started. The hideout was sited on the Downs at the base of a steep wooded slope in the western part of Kingley Vale, to the north of West Ashling. Sited further up the slope beside a bridleway was the patrol's lookout, which commanded a view

37. West Ashling Patrol underground lookout, now collapsed but with its two foot square entrance shaft of corrugated iron still in place.

across the valley below and was connected to the hideout via a direct telephone line. Its entrance hatch was attached to a tree root sticking out of the ground. On lifting this the hatch would open, assisted by a counterbalance weight. In the bottom of the valley was an underground store for extra food and ammunition. All the three underground sites are thought to have been built by the Royal Engineers.

Stanley Mason's son Bob recalled the time his father's patrol were asked for volunteers to be parachuted into France as a pre-invasion plan. The men declined, considering themselves unsuitable for such an ambitious assault.

Wiston Patrol

This patrol was made up of six members. The Patrol Leader was Jack Webley, a farmer at Fairoak Farm, Wiston. The other members were John Heath, a farmer at Muntham Farm on Findon Downs; Burt Dean, a gamekeeper to the Wiston estate shoot, who lived in a cottage on Fairoak Farm; Jack Grange, a land agent to the Wiston Estate, who lived in Shirley House, Wiston; Wilfred How, a farmer from near Wiston Park, described as a small jockey-like man; and John Scragg, a schoolmaster from Steyning. The latter was chosen as a patrol member because of his excellent knowledge of the surrounding area due to taking his pupils on numerous field trips.

All the men did their basic training at Coleshill House and continued localised training in and around Wiston. Jack Webley is known to have gone to Scotland to take part in special training: he is thought to be the only patrol member to do this kind of long-distance training.

The patrol's hideout is said to have been sited in a small wood to the north of Chanctonbury Ring, near the bottom of the Downs escarpment but, because the patrol kept its exact whereabouts so secret, no-one knows for sure. The patrol also had what has been termed a 'forward store'. This underground store was sited near the top of a chalk pit on the Downs west of the river Adur, near a farm called 'Coombes', and was built by the Royal Engineers. It was positioned close to the chalk pit so that the spoil from the excavation could be thrown directly and unnoticeably amongst the other chalk. This store measured 12 feet square and 8 feet high, with a small camouflaged hatch as an entrance. It would have contained extra supplies of food, ammunition and explosives. The patrol, in this area, could have used equipment out of this 'forward store' rather than carrying it all from their OB. The store remained fully stocked until well after the war, and was regularly checked to ensure everything was in good order.

John Scragg's wife Jean related her husband's involvement with the Auxiliary Units. She remembered him blacking up his face before going out for a night of training with the patrol. Soon after he had gone out, she would hear various explosions from the patrol's activities in the area.

Buried in the side of the road leading into Steyning were some 50 gallon oil drums filled with an inflammable mixture. These had a small explosive charge and a fuse attached to them. The patrol would be responsible for detonating these drums when a German convoy was passing through.

Jean Scragg still had her husband's Home Guard titles - Sussex shoulder flashes and the battalion number 203 that were sewn onto his uniform - along with the stand-down letters he received.

SUSSEX PATROLS - RESEARCH STATISTICS

PATROLS & MEN

Total number of patrols = 23
Total number of men = 139
Average number to a patrol = 6

OCCUPATIONS

Farmers	68
Others (made up of 20 different occupations)	24
Farm Workers	13
Market Gardeners & Gardeners	8
Gamekeepers	7
Agricultural Engineers	6
Forestry Commission	4
Woodcutters	3
Builders	3
Unknown	3

Total   139 men

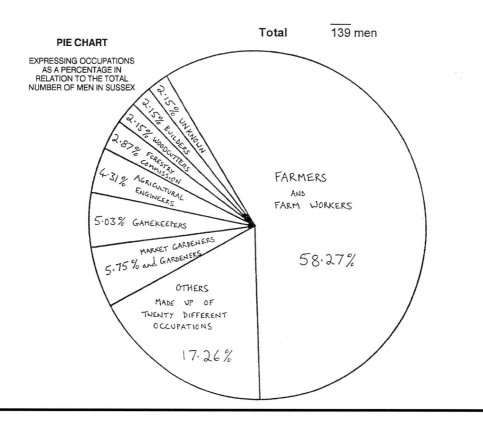

PIE CHART

EXPRESSING OCCUPATIONS
AS A PERCENTAGE IN
RELATION TO THE TOTAL
NUMBER OF MEN IN SUSSEX

2.15% UNKNOWN
2.15% BUILDERS
2.15% WOODCUTTERS
2.87% FORESTRY COMMISSION
4.31% AGRICULTURAL ENGINEERS
5.03% GAMEKEEPERS
5.75% MARKET GARDENERS and GARDENERS

FARMERS
AND
FARM WORKERS

58.27%

OTHERS
MADE UP OF
TWENTY DIFFERENT
OCCUPATIONS

17.26%

PART THREE

THE THREAT OF INVASION

5. OPERATION SEA LION

The build up to the German invasion of Britain started on the night of 13 August 1940 with a propoganda stunt. The Luftwaffe dropped a large number of parachutes along with various other pieces of equipment in the Midlands to give the impression of an invading party. Despite a thorough search no troops were found.

Four German spies were successfully parachuted into Kent on 3 September 1940, but were soon captured. After these men were interrogated it was found they were an advance guard for the invasion, which according to them was to take place in the near future. By the evening of 7 September intelligence sources were confident an invasion was imminent and issued the code-word 'CROMWELL', which meant the invasion had started, and military units all over Britain braced themselves for an invasion which was not in fact occurring.

The German invasion, code named Operation Sealion, was planned to take place between 19 September and 26 September 1940. Its aim was to capture Southern England within the first ten days, London shortly afterwards, and the whole of Britain within a month. The main assault would have taken place along the Kent and Sussex coastline. The invading troops in Sussex would have been made up of the 9th and 16th Armies. Divisions from these had the following objectives:

The 7th Division and 1st Mountain Division were to land at Camber Sands, Rye and Winchelsea Beach, respectively, and make towards Hawkhurst.

The 34th Division and the 26th Division would land at Bexhill and Pevensey, respectively, and make towards Uckfield.

The 6th Division would land at the River Cuckmere's haven and follow the river until past Alfriston then turn west towards Ringmer.

The 8th Division would have landed at Rottingdean making towards Burgess Hill. It is thought that paratroopers would have been dropped into designated areas to assist all the aforementioned divisions.

From this information it can be seen that all these landings would have taken place in East Sussex. This was mainly due to its position next to Kent (which afforded the shortest cross-channel route to the invaders) and the suitability of its beaches for landing troops, horses and equipment. Newhaven, with its harbour, would have been used for the unloading of supplies in the days after the initial invasion. All the Sussex Patrols would have been in a position to put their training to good use had Operation Sealion been implemented.

For the Germans the English Channel was the biggest barrier to overcome. Tides and unpredictable weather conditions, unsuitable (improvised) landing craft, coupled with the Luftwaffe's failure to weaken the RAF, would have made the enterprise fraught with danger for the troops involved long before they had reached the beaches. Accordingly the invasion plan was abandoned and Hitler turned his attention to Russia.

One point of interest is that the Germans knew that all the signposts, milestones, street names, railway station and village names had been taken down. They were prepared for this and had produced cloth signs with place-names already painted on and others that were left blank. These were to be put up by advance pathfinders to show the invading troops which way to go.

As late as April 1941 Hitler still had plans being made for an invasion of Britain. This was called Operation Shark and was a revised version of Sealion.

The only German invasion that this country ever witnessed was that of its prisoners of war, who by 1942 started arriving in large numbers. The POWs were held in camps, usually set up on racecourses and football grounds, scattered throughout the British Isles. These sites were chosen because they were easily guarded and their ability to hold large numbers of men. By the end of the War there were over a quarter of a million German POWs in this country.

In early December 1944 the Germans hoped to capitalise on this resident ready made army. A remarkably elaborate plan for a mass breakout was initiated, the directive coming from mainland Germany. On escaping these men were to try to arm themselves with whatever they could lay their hands on, then make for London. Many did escape, however, not in the huge numbers that had been hoped for. Some within the camps had informed on the plan and security was stepped up. Consequently the whole operation failed miserably.

6. LIFE EXPECTANCY IN THE EVENT OF AN INVASION.

All the former Auxiliary Unit members interviewed were under no illusion as to their fate if an invasion had taken place. They knew, as individual patrols, they would be on their own hoping to cause much havoc and destruction to any established German installations as well as communications and supply lines. Once the Germans had realised that resistance groups were in operation searches would have been made of surrounding areas. Tracker dogs would have been the main threat of detection, especially if a whole patrol were inside their underground hideout.

If they had lived longer than the predicted two week life expectancy of a patrol their food supplies would have soon run out. The need to trap or steal food may well have given the whereabouts of the patrol away quicker than their sabotage activities.

Reprisals for the sabotage attacks would probably have taken a similar form to those carried out in Europe, in an attempt to find the whereabouts of clandestine operatives. Local people were picked at random, lined up and shot by a firing squad. Sometimes larger massacres occured, such as the one carried out by the infamous SS Das Reich Division in France in 1944. These terror tactics, occurring day after day, would have put enormous pressure on the people who knew of a patrol's whereabouts, as well as on patrol members themselves. They would know that friends and relatives could be slaughtered because of their activities.

The outstanding point from all the interviews with former members of the Auxiliary Units is that they believed in what they were doing and that they had the potential to cause considerable damage to any invading Germans.

How would a modern day version of a British underground resistance fare fifty years on? Plastic high explosive would still be its main weapon, more than likely using an electronic remote control to detonate it rather than the mechanical devices used in the past (see Appendix A). The patrols would be up against sophisticated detection equipment such as infra-red cameras, security lights and night sights that could pick up men moving about at night. Thermal Imaging Equipment used in a helicopter could find an underground hideout full of men by the radiation given off by their body heat.

It seems the years have favoured the protection by detection approach to sabotage attacks whatever their purpose. Different tactics would be required, such as those used by the IRA in the recent past, to have even limited success. Equipment could be hidden in secret caches, but the men themselves would have to fade into the general population.

7. STAND DOWN

On 18th November 1944 the General Commander in Chief, H.E. Franklyn, sent a letter to the Colonel Commander of the Auxiliary Units, F.W.R. Douglas, informing him to advise all the members of the Auxiliary Units of the official opinion from the War Office that it was time to stand down the operations side.

The letter read as follows:

```
The Commander GHQ Auxiliary Units
```

In view of the improved war situation, it has been decided by the War Office that the operational Branch of Auxiliary Units shall stand down, and the time has now come to put an end to an organisation which would have been of inestimable value to this country in the event of invasion.

All ranks under your command are aware of the secret nature of their duties. For that reason it has not been possible for them to receive publicity, nor will it be possible even now. So far from considering this to be a misfortune, I should like all members of Auxiliary Units to regard this as a matter of special pride. I have been much impressed by the devotion to duty and high standard of training shown by all ranks. The careful preparations, the hard work undertaken in their own time and their readiness to face the inevitable dangers of their role, are all matters which reflect the greatest credit on the body of picked men who form the Auxiliary Units.

I should be glad, therefore, if my congratulations and best wishes could be conveyed to all ranks.

```
  (signed) H.E. Franklyn General Commander in Chief
                           GHQ Home Forces 18th November 1944.
```

On 30 November Colonel Douglas sent the letter of notification to all Auxiliary Unit members informing them of the decision to stand down the units. Attached to this was a copy of the Commander-in-Chief's aforementioned letter.

The letter of notification read as follows:

```
From: Colonel F.W.R. Douglas
To:   The members of Auxiliary Units - Operational Branch

The War Office has ordered that the Operational side of Auxiliary Units shall
stand down!  This is due to the greatly improved War situation and the strategic
requirements of the moment.
```

I realise what joining the Auxiliary Units has meant to you; so do the officers under my command. You were invited to do a job which would require more skill and coolness, more hard work and greater danger, than was demanded of any other voluntary organisation. In the event of "Action Stations" being ordered you knew well the kind of life you were in for. But that was in order; you were picked men; and others, including myself, knew that you would continue to fight whatever the conditions, with, or if necessary without, orders.

It now falls to me to tell you that your work has been appreciated and well carried out, and that your contract, for the moment, is at an end. I am grateful to you for the way you have trained in the last four years. So is the Regular Army. It was due to you that more divisions left this country to fight the battle of France; and it was due to your reputation for skill and determination that extra risk was taken - successfully as it turned out - in the defence arrangements of this country during that vital period. I congratulate you on this reputation and thank you for this voluntary effort.

In view of the fact that your lives depended on secrecy no public recognition will be possible. But those in the responsible positions at General Headquarters, Home Forces, know what was done and what would have been done had you been called upon. They know it well, as is emphasised in the attached letter from the Commander-in-Chief. It will not be forgotten.

Frank W.R. Douglas
Colonel Commander,
Auxiliary Units
30 NOV 44
C/o G.P.O. Highworth
Nr. Swindon (Wilts).

After notification of the Auxiliary Units' disbandment all the patrols returned their weapons, explosives and other equipment to various designated pick-up points.

Later all the men were presented with a commemorative lapel badge. This was metal and made in the shape of a small shield measuring three-quarters of an inch (2cm) high and five-eighths of an inch (1.6cm) across. Its design had been well thought out and took into account the three battalions 201, 202 and 203 that had existed around the country. The men also received a certificate, this was the same as the regular Home Guard received and stated:

"In the years when our Country was in mortal danger this man gave generously of his time and powers to make himself ready for her defence by force of arms and with his life if need be."

It was signed by King George but made no mention of their involvement in the Auxiliary Units.

8. CONCLUSION

It is easy now to look back over the documented war years and realise that any real threat of a German invasion subsided after October 1940. However, during the War it was not until 1943 that a more relaxed attitude towards the so-called 'invasion' of this country came about.

The Auxiliary Units were formed when the threat of an invasion seemed very real and, whilst the whole operation was totally organised, time was initially the limiting factor as to how many patrols could be effectively formed.

The men who made up these patrols were quite unique, volunteering for what can only be described as a suicide mission, but volunteer they did. These men were either too old to be called up into the forces or were in reserved occupations. They went beyond the duties and responsibilities of the regular Home Guard to become Britain's first underground resistance movement. At the time they were not to know that this would be their only accolade.

We can only speculate as to the outcome of their activities had they ever been put into practice, yet all the men were highly trained, superbly equipped and greatly motivated by the cause for which they were formed.

38. The commemorative lapel badge issued at the end of the auxiliary units operational years. The top two-thirds has a red background with the remaining part being blue.

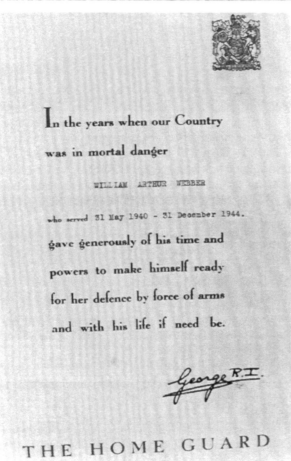

I n the years when our Country

was in mortal danger

WILLIAM ARTHUR WEBBER

who served 31 May 1940 - 31 December 1944.

gave generously of his time and

powers to make himself ready

for her defence by force of arms

and with his life if need be.

George R.I.

THE HOME GUARD

39. Bill Webbers standard issue Home Guard certificate. Even though he was in actual fact the Firle Patrol Leader and was a member of the auxiliary units, throughout their operational years, it makes no mention of this.

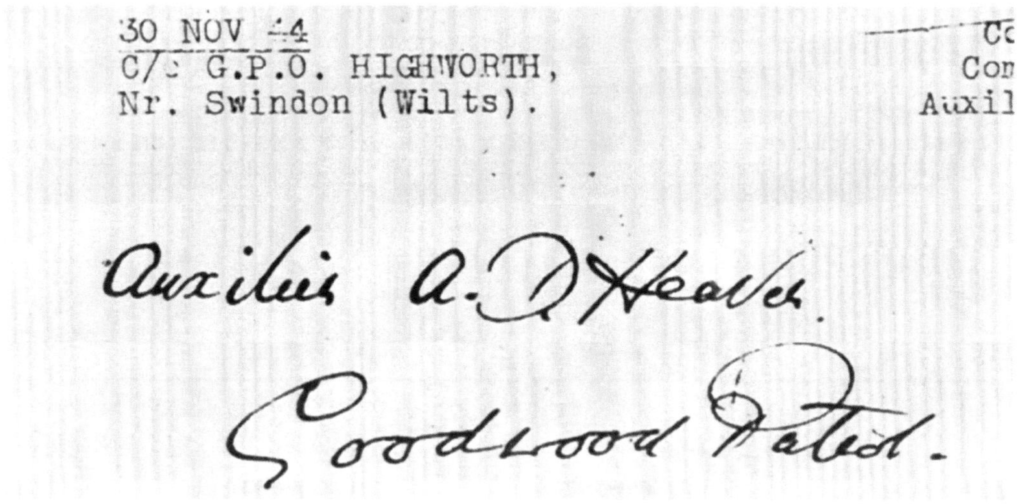

```
30 NOV  4                                    C
C/  G.P.O. HIGHWORTH,                      Con
Nr. Swindon (Wilts).                      Auxil
```

Auxilii A. D Heaver.

Goodwood Patrol.

40. Alan Heaver's name and patrol title written at the bottom of his stand down letter. The writing is believed to be that of Small Dole patrol leader George Cooper, the man responsible for the winding up of the West Sussex Patrols.

Winston Churchill always showed great interest in the Auxiliary Units and was of the opinion they were a useful addition to the regular forces. It may or may not be a coincidence that the Auxiliary Unit Patrols were stood down on 30 November - his birthday. Colin Gubbins considered the formation of the Auxiliary Units a personal achievement to be proud of and, as far as he was concerned, designed and trained for a specific role that would have justified their existence by costing the country nothing in manpower or equipment.

Within the standown letter it states the men of the auxiliary units "will not be forgotten". However, without any official records being released until the year 2020 it is more the case of will anyone remember them.

It was a privilege to have met former members of the Auxiliary Units, who in turn revealed information never told before, considering my research timely in respect of their dwindling numbers. Hopefully, at last, these men will gain the recognition that they deserve for being the best kept secret of the Second World War.

Finally, although not in Sussex, a recently made discovery is worth mentioning. In 1978 a bridge near Margate in Kent was found to have plastic explosive still attached to it, long forgotten by the local Auxiliary Unit patrol who originally placed it there! One may speculate on how many other secrets have yet to be discovered about the Home Guard Auxiliary Units.

41. Bill Webber and the author organised a reunion of the ex. Sussex Patrol members to celebrate 50 years since their stand down. This took place on 30th November 1994 at Tottington Manor, the old regional headquarters. From left to right:- Ex. member but not in Sussex name unknown, Frank Mayston (Royal Engineers), Arthur Gabbitas (Signals), Tom Smith (Firle Patrol), Bill Webber (Firle Patrol Leader), Ex. member but not in Sussex name unknown, George Thomas (Ditchling Patrol Leader), Alan Cooke (Icklesham Patrol), Ronald Peel (Stansted Patrol), Frank Penfold (Arundel Patrol Leader), Ex. member but not in Sussex name unknown, George Huxham (Stansted Patrol), Eric Johnson (Ashburnham Patrol), Ex. Female member but not in Sussex name unknown, Geoffrey Bradford (ex. member in Devon, partially obscured), Sidney Gaston (Royal Sussex Regiment), John Richards (Hellingly Patrol Leader) and Colin Cooke (Icklesham Patrol).

APPENDIX A

EQUIPMENT

EQUIPMENT

All the men in the Auxiliary Unit patrols were issued with regular Home Guard uniforms and kit, but unlike the regular Home Guard they were far better equipped with weapons and explosives. The following lists were given to all Sussex Patrol Leaders itemising the equipment issued to the men as well as stores to be kept by the Patrol Leader. Advice was also given on storing equipment.

Personal equipment and side arms

Each patrol member's kit comprised:

PISTOL .38 or .32	1	BRUSH OR ROD (CLEANING PISTOL)	1
AMMUNITION .38 or .32	36/40	BATTLEDRESS TROUSERS	1
BATTLE DRESS BLOUSE	1	BOOTS	1pr
FORAGE CAP	1	OVERCOAT D M	1
LACES	1	LEATHER ANKLETS	1pr
PISTOL HOLSTER, WEBBING or LEATHER	1	FIELD DRESSING	1
BELT, WEBBING or LEATHER	1	BLANKETS G S	2
GAS MASK COMPLETE	1	HAVERSACK, WEBBING	1
EYESHIELDS pkt of 6	1	DENIM BLOUSE WITH BUTTONS	1
DENIM TROUSERS	1	STERILIZATION SETS	2
TITLES - HOMEGUARD	4	NUMERALS 203	4
BRACE - HAVERSACK	1	STEEL HELMET	1
GLOVES	1	LANYARD	1
RUBBER TRUNCHEON	1	RUBBER ANKLE BOOTS	1pr
FLASHES - SUSSEX	6	CAP BADGE	1
CAMOUFLAGE VEIL	1	KNIFE	1
FORK	1	SPOON	1
MESS TIN	1	FIGHTING KNIFE	1
GROUND SHEET	1	BOX OF OINTMENT A G No 2	1

The pistol with which the men were issued was often of American origin, usually either a .38 calibre Smith & Wesson or a .32 calibre Colt automatic.

The fighting knife was more commonly known as a 'Fairbairn Dagger'. Its construction was of solid steel and it had a seven inch blade made by Wilkinson Sword. The knife gets its name from its designer Lieutenant Colonel W F Fairbairn who was a member of the Shanghai Police Force in the 1930's. He was an expert in close combat, pistol shooting and various martial arts. He went on to establish the commando methods of unarmed combat.

Denims were generally worn for training, as were the rubber boots that were ideal for silent movement.

The rubber truncheons were simply a straight piece of extruded black rubber rod 14½ inches long, into which some men hammered metal studs for greater effect.

The official battalion title was 203 GHQ (RESERVE) Bn HOME GUARD. Therefore, the men were issued with Home Guard titles, Sussex flashes and the 203 numerals to be sewn onto their uniforms. The 203 numerals always prompted many questions, as people had never heard of this battalion.

42. The 'Fairbairn Dagger' had a double edge 7" blade and was issued with a sheath that could be attached to a belt, elastic straps holding it tight to the leg. The knuckleduster although not a standard issue found its way into many members personal kit.

43. Initially the auxiliary units were issued with a bulky and heavy wooden truncheon, nearly two feet long with metal studs hammered into it. The insert photo shows how lead was poured into a bore hole to add extra weight.

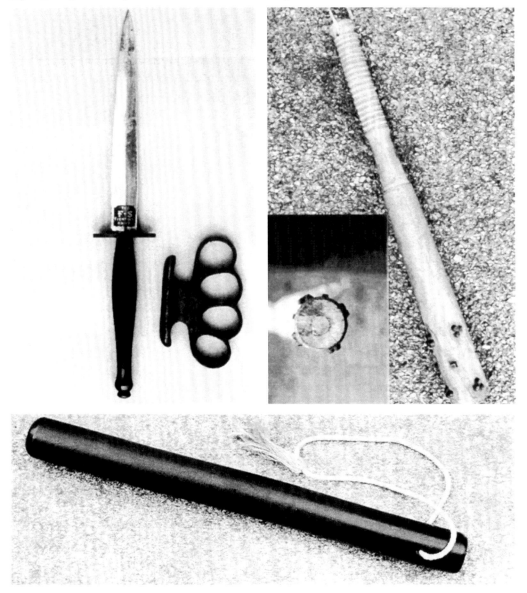

44. A shorter rubber truncheon soon replaced the unsuitable wooden one. Being only 14" long it was much easier to carry slipping neatly into the uniforms trouser pocket.

45. Home Guard Title, Sx (Sussex) Flashes and Battalion Numerals 203. These would have been sewn on both arms of the uniform in the order as shown.

Small arms

Stores held at Patrol Leader's house:

RIFLES .300	2	RIFLES SLING	2
THOMPSON SUB-MACHINE GUN	1	THOMPSON SMG MAGAZINES	10
THOMPSON SMG SLING	1	BOX W/CLEANING BRUSHES - THOMPSON SMG	1
STEN GUNS	4	STEN GUN MAGAZINES	up to 32 per patrol
STEN GUN FILLERS	4	STEN GUN SLINGS	4
PULL THROUGHS	6	OIL BOTTLES	6
GAUZES	10	RUM	1 Gallon
.22 RIFLE WITH ROD	1	TELEPHONES	2
CELLS FOR TELEPHONE	4	GOGGLES N P	3pr

Only two .300 calibre rifles were issued to each patrol. These do not appear to have been a memorable item of equipment as no one interviewed could recall the manufacturer's name. However, they were probably Springfield rifles from America, released from First World War stocks, hence their unusual calibre.

Everyone's favourite weapon was the Thompson sub-machine gun, also American. It weighed approximately ten and a half pounds and fired a .45 calibre bullet at a rate of 800 rounds per minute. Two types of magazine were issued, depending on availability. These were either a 20 round box or a 50 round drum. The gun is usually associated with American gangsters of the 1930s, who favoured the longer-lasting drum magazine.

The British Sten Gun was more readily available and more commonly used in training. It weighed 7lbs and fired a 9mm calibre bullet at a rate of 500 rounds per minute. It used a 32 round box magazine. The Sten Gun was notorious for either jamming after just one shot or letting the whole magazine fire in one long burst. Cleaning was advised every ten days whether the gun had been used or not.

The .22 calibre rifle issued was a specialised Winchester model 74 from America. This was a semi-automatic rifle that was modified with a Hale-Parker silencer and a mounting for a telescopic sight. The weapon was reputed to have a range of up to a mile and was intended for sniping.

Each Patrol was given a gallon jar of rum. This was to be used to keep the men's spirits up if the Germans invaded. Although it was advised to keep this at the Patrol Leader's house, it was more often than not kept in the Patrol's hideout.

Explosives

THE FOLLOWING STORES SHOULD BE AT THE O.B.:

GRENADES 36M	48	BOTTLES A.W.		48
AUX UNITS MkII	15	RELEASE SWITCHES		50
COMPASS MAGNETIC	1	PULL SWITCHES		50
TYRE CUTTER	1	PRESSURE SWITCHES		50
SPARE DETONATORS	50	PARAFFIN	up to 10 gals. per patrol	
FIRST AID SET	1	THERMOMETER		1
MONOCULAR AND CASE	1	SHELL DRESSINGS	up to 4 per patrol	
PRIMUS STOVE	1	TELEPLHONE CABLE	already laid	
LAMPS HURRICANE	2	PLASTIC H.E.	up to 30lb per patrol	
PICK AND HELVE	1	L. DELAYS 1hr - 15)	unless L.Delays for	
POUCHES BASIC	2	L. DELAYS 3hr - 15)	Aux.unit MkII have	
		)	been issued	
SHOVELS	2	COTTON WASTE		½lb
DET. CARRIERS	8	CRIMPING TOOLS		4
M.E.B.	48	C.T.I. (where issued)		60
ELSAN AND ELSANOL	1	STRIKER BOARDS		24
TRIPWIRE ROLLS	24	MAGNETS		24
TRAPWIRE ROLLS	24	TIME PENCILS (where issued)		240
AMMUNITION .450	1200	CAMOUFLAGE CREAM		3 black
" 9mm	1250	" "		3 green
" .300	100	" "		3 brown
" .22	200			

The detonators supplied were small aluminium tubes about 2 inches long by one eighth of an inch wide and open at one end. They contained a very sensitive high explosive which would explode when heated. They could be used to explode charges of high explosive, fired by safety fuse or Orange Line. The fuse would be inserted in the open end and crimped in place.

Safety fuse, although not mentioned on the list, must have been available for use with the detonators and copper tube igniters (CTI). Safety fuse looks like dark grey insulated wire, its core being gunpowder. It is a slow burning fuse and burns at a rate of two feet per minute. The best method of lighting it is with a match. The CTI would have had a match placed inside it and it would then be crimped to the end of the fuse. This in turn would have been struck on the striker board.

Orange Line is a faster burning fuse filled with a greater amount of gunpowder and burns at a rate of 90 feet per second. This would never be started with a match. Instead a short length of safety fuse would have been used to ignite it.

High explosives were available in three different forms: plastic, gelignite and Noble's Explosive 808. Plastic explosive was issued to the Auxiliary Units long before it was made available to the regular army. High explosives are unstable materials which when ignited by a detonator turn into a gas at a high temperature and pressure. Most of this pressure is lost to the surrounding air, but can be used if the explosive charge has a heavy material placed around it. This is known as 'tamping'. The faster it explodes, the quicker it will turn into a gas. To achieve this, the charge needs to have a high speed explosive placed next to it. This is known as 'priming'.

Cordtex, another item not on the list, was available and could be used, among other things, as a primer for the three explosives. Cordtex was a thin, white plastic tube filled with high explosive. It was flexible to a certain degree, and could only be exploded with a detonator. It could be used to connect two or more charges in a circuit, only using one detonator, so that they would explode at the same time. Cordtex detonates very fast, at approximately 6,000 metres per second.

Plastic high explosive has been described as the finest general explosive in the world. It is a very fast explosive, dull yellow or black in colour with a putty-like consistency. It was made up of 4oz sticks wrapped in cellophane or greaseproof paper. The plastic here could be softened by adding Vaseline which was supplied in toothpaste tubes. It could be used as an explosive on its own or to prime other explosives. Being plastic, it could be moulded around any object and stored in damp conditions without being affected. It would also not deteriorate with age.

Gelignite was a slower explosive but more readily available. It was buff or greyish-brown in colour and made in 4 or 8oz sticks wrapped in thick waxed paper. Unprimed, it had a detonating speed of approximately 2,500 metres per second, but, when primed, was four times more powerful. Gelignite, when unwrapped, could not be touched with bare hands as it caused a headache equal to a hangover. It was therefore impractical to mould gelignite to any target. It would have had to be taped or tied. It could also be taped to the magnets supplied, and thus attached to a metal target. Gelignite suffers badly from damp storage.

Noble's Explosive 808 was a very tough, light buff coloured jelly with a strong smell of almond oil. It was made up in 4 oz sticks wrapped in thin waxed paper. It could be used in exactly the same way as gelignite but, unlike gelignite, it did not suffer from damp storage.

All these explosive stores needed to be examined at least once a fortnight.

Two sorts of delay mechanism for explosive charges were supplied. These were the time pencil and the L-Delay. The time pencil derived its name from its similarity to a propelling pencil. It contained a glass phial full of cupric chloride, a corrosive fluid. When this phial was broken, the fluid would come into contact with a steel wire. It would eat through the wire, eventually releasing a spring which pushed a striker onto the percussion cap. This caused a flash which fired the detonator, exploding the charge.

The cupric chloride came in different strengths which varied the amount of delay. The time pencils were colour-coded: red for half hour, white for one and a half hours, green for five hours, yellow for ten hours and blue for twenty hours delay respectively. These delay times were governed by temperature, so the delay would be longer in winter since the acid worked more slowly in the cold.

The L-Delay, or Lead Delay, was so called because it used the tension of a spring to pull on an element made of lead. This did away with a chemical reaction. The spring would gradually stretch the metal until it broke, releasing the striker onto the cap in the same way as the time pencil. Different delays were achieved by using a different thickness of lead element. Like the time pencils, the L-Delays resembled a propelling pencil, but were thicker. These, too, were affected by temperature.

Tables were issued with both kinds of delay to help calculate the difference between summer and winter delay times. Both these delays could fire a safety fuse, Orange Line or a detonator.

Grenade 36M, or Mills Grenade, was more commonly known as the 'hand grenade'. It weighed one and a half pounds and could be thrown for a distance of about thirty five yards. Before throwing, the safety pin had to be removed. To do this, it was advised that the grenade should always be pulled away from the pin. Once thrown, the grenade had a four-second delay before exploding. Accuracy in throwing was far more important than distance.

Another grenade available was the No. 77 Smoke Grenade. This weighed three quarters of a pound and contained white phosphorus. When it exploded, the phosphorus ignited and gave off dense smoke for about thirty seconds.

An AW bottle was an incendiary device also called an SIP or Self-Igniting Phosphorus bottle. It was a half pint clear glass bottle containing yellow phosphorus and rubber dissolved in benzol. When the bottle was broken, the contents burst into flame, giving off a dense cloud of foul-smelling smoke. If the fire was put out with water, it would start up again as soon as the water dried. This weapon would have been used as a fire and smoke grenade in an ambush on vehicles.

Other incendiary devices available were the Magnesium Incendiary, a Fire Pot, and the Pocket Time Incendiary. These were all suitable for destroying combustible stores or petrol dumps, because they burned with an extremely hot flame. They could all be set off with a time delay fuse.

The pull switch and the pressure switch were both mechanisms to be used in booby traps. The pull switch would have worked via a trap or trip wire. Trap wire was 0.01 inches thick and was used for short distances, whereas the trip wire was 0.032 inches thick and was capable of tripping a fourteen stone man who was running. This was used for covering greater distances. The wire was attached to the release pin on the end of the pull switch. When a pull of more than four pounds was applied to the end of the wire, the spring-loaded striker was released, setting off the percussion cap and, light the Orange Line fuse, detonating the explosive charge. The switch had an anchor leg to allow it to be firmly secured to a tree trunk or fence post.

The pressure switch could have been used against vehicles as well as foot soldiers. It would have been buried, just leaving the top of its shearing pin level with the ground, making it easy to camouflage. The switch worked when a pressure of more than forty pounds was applied to the shearing pin. This then cut through the striker spindle and released the spring-loaded striker, allowing it to set off the percussing cap, light the fuse and detonate the charge.

The release switch worked in the opposite way to the pressure switch. It needed to have a weight put on top of it, such as a trap door. When this weight was removed, it released the striker, setting off the charge in the same way as the pull and pressure switches.

Another available weapon, not included in the list, was the ST Grenade or 'sticky bomb'. This form of hand grenade was intended for use against armoured vehicles. The bomb's core was one and a half pounds of explosive charge surrounded by an adhesive covering, and the whole assembly was contained inside a glass flask. When the pin was pulled and the grenade thrown, a five second fuse would start. On impact with the armoured vehicle, the glass flask would break, leaving the grenade stuck to the armour plating, making the explosion very effective.

Lastly, small hook-shaped knives, very sharp and capable of slicing through the side wall of a tyre, were issued. These were similar to the ones used by Special Operations Executive (SOE) operatives.

SOE operatives were given cyanide tablets for use in case of capture. However, Auxiliary Unit patrols were not issued with these. They had morphine in their first aid kits. Not only could this be used for its pain-relieving qualities, but a large enough dose would have proved fatal.

From this list, it can be seen that all the Sussex patrols had both modern and sophisticated weapons at their disposal. These, combined with their training, would have made them a force of saboteurs to be reckoned with.

46. Internal view of a Pressure Switch taken from the auxiliary unit training manual.

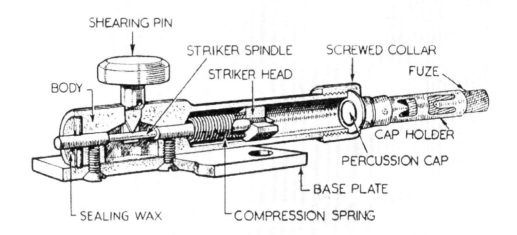

PRESSURE SWITCH

47. Taken again from the training manual the internal view of the Pull Switch.

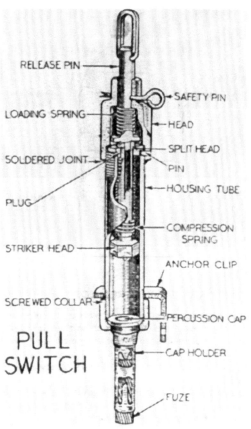

RELEASE PIN

SAFETY PIN

LOADING SPRING

HEAD

SPLIT HEAD

SOLDERED JOINT

PIN

HOUSING TUBE

PLUG

COMPRESSION SPRING

STRIKER HEAD

ANCHOR CLIP

SCREWED COLLAR

PERCUSSION CAP

PULL SWITCH

CAP HOLDER

FUZE

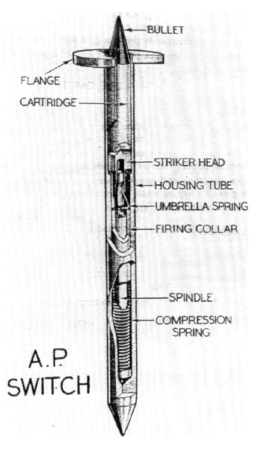

BULLET

FLANGE

CARTRIDGE

STRIKER HEAD

HOUSING TUBE

UMBRELLA SPRING

FIRING COLLAR

SPINDLE

COMPRESSION SPRING

A.P. SWITCH

48. Drawing explaining all the parts that make up an Anti-Personnel Switch.

APPENDIX B

RELATED ORGANISATIONS

SPECIAL DUTIES ORGANISATION

This section of the Auxiliary Units was formed after the sabotage side of the resistance had already been established. Its members were never told of the many patrols in existence all around the country. The Special Duties Organisation's role involved communications (radio) and spying. The headquarters for the unit was located at Hannington Hall, Hannington, Wiltshire, just five miles from Coleshill House. The section's personnel consisted of spies, cut-outs, out-station radio operators and the people who would operate the control and zero stations.

Unlike the sabotage-minded patrols both men and women could be chosen for the task of spying. The main people recruited for this role were people whose jobs allowed plenty of movement - doctors, midwives, postmen, vicars and farm workers. These people were trained separately in their own areas, being taught how to make simple intelligence reports. In the event of a German invasion they would have carried on their usual business or routine, making reports of any German troop movements, or anything else of interest they had observed. Once a report was completed the spy needed to pass the information on to a radio operator. This was achieved by use of a secret 'letter box'. This could take many forms. For instance an old tin can, or hole in a tree or under a rock could be adopted. All that was required was a place where the report could be hidden and be accessible to the radio operator.

If the radio operator did not pick up the report himself, someone known as a 'cut-out' would pick it up and transfer it to a second secret letter box where it could be retrived for transmission. The use of this system kept the identity of the spies and cut-outs from the radio-operators and vice-versa.

A radio operator along with his equipment was classified as an out-station. The radio's whereabouts had to be kept totally secret. This was achieved by siting most of the radios in underground hideouts. The radio used by the Special Duties Organisation was purpose built to be basic in design and simple to use. They were built by the Royal Corps of Signals men working on a production line at Coleshill. The radio sets measured approximately 15 inches long, 6 inches high and 5 inches wide. They worked on the, then rarely used, frequency between 60 and 65 megacycles that was probably not even monitored by the Germans. A six volt car battery was used to power the radio set. This needed a 40 feet long aerial to be able to transmit its messages.

Had the Germans landed the radio operators would have carried on with their normal occupations, only visiting their out-stations to transmit short reports of information. These out-station operators would all be transmitting to their local control stations, of which Sussex had three. The purpose of a control station was to relay information gained from the various out-stations back to headquarters at Hannington Hall.

A control station was operated by three specially trained women of the ATS Auxiliary Unit, each station having two transmitters and two recievers. One set was for everyday use whilst the whole radio network was in training, the other to be used in the event of an invasion. The training set was often housed in a surface building. The other set would have been close by in an underground hideout known as a 'zero station', so-called because when the station's code-name was used it was always followed by the code suffix 'zero'. There were no transmitting schedules for the out-station operators to keep so the women would have to listen for messages coming in for long stretches of time. Once a message had been decoded the information would have been telephoned, via a direct phone line, to Hannington Hall.

Information about the Special Duties Organisation in Sussex is sparse and in some ways has remained more secretive since the War than the sabotage side of the Auxiliary Units. It was only possible to interview two former members of the organisation and it has been neccessary to rely heavily on information provided by the relatives of former members.

East Sussex

In East Sussex the only member located was Harold West. He was a farmer at Bevendean Farm near Brighton and joined the organisation as a radio operator. Initially his set was hidden in an underground hideout on the outskirts of Telscombe village. However, this was discovered by a poacher who sat on the tree stump that was attached to the entrance hatch. The stump wobbled and fell over revealing the hideout beneath. Being very suspicious he reported his find to the police and the hideout had to be abandonded. The radio set was moved to a new underground site within the vicarage garden at Telscombe beside the church. Again after a short time this second site was discovered prompting serious allegations about the vicar being a spy for the Germans! It has not been established whether he was a spy within the Special Duties Organisation or not but it is certainly a possibility. After this drawback it was decided the radio should be moved out of the Telscombe area and it was re-located in another underground site within Half Moon Wood near St Mary's Farm, Falmer. Lawrence Pye, the farmer at St Mary's Farm, also became a radio operator and shared the use of the set with Harold West. The site proved to be a good choice as its whereabouts was never discovered throughout its use. It is known the men had a contact at Clayton along with another in Lewes, a Dr Sinclair. Unfortunately Harold West is now deceased.

Other out-station radio operators in East Sussex include Edwin Trangmere, a farmer at Priesthawes House, near Stone Cross. He had his radio set hidden in an underground hideout within his garden. The hideout was constructed entirely of wood and measured aproximately 10 feet long, 5 feet wide and 8 feet high. It contained a table to sit the radio on along with its battery and a chair for the operator. Entrance was gained by lifting an earth-covered wooden hatch and climbing down a wooden ladder. An emergency exit tunnel went out under the garden wall, emerging the other side in a field. The radio's aerial ran up one of the big elm trees in the garden.

Edwin's son Andrew Trangmere can recall that every time his father went down into the hideout his three dogs would sit down on the entrance hatch waiting for their master to come out again! Andrew's role was to note down any troop movements he saw along the Stone Cross to Hailsham road, putting this information into a split tennis ball. He would then roll the ball down one of the ventilation pipes of the hideout for his father to transmit as a coded message.

Sydney Dinnis, a farmer at Parkwood Farm, Upper Dicker kept his radio set inside a cupboard within a locked room of the farmhouse. In 1943 he moved to Priory Farm, Wilmington, continuing as a radio operator from this new location. The radio was again hidden within the farmhouse, its aerial going up the inside of the chimney.

Dr Stuart Hogg, who lived in Westham, near to Pevensey Castle, had his set contained within a small briefcase which gave mobility to his transmissions, although he did have a permanent aerial running up a tree in his garden. He is believed to have been in charge of the Pevensey and surrounding area radio operators. Mr Allen of the Lamb Inn, Wartling and Mr Ade from Ciderford Lane, near Cowbeech, were both radio operators.

Henry Thomsett, a gamekeeper in Crowhurst Park, Telham just outside Battle, shared his radio transmitter with a Mr Calder, a farmer from Breadsell Farm, Telham. The radio was sited in an underground hideout within nearby Ring Wood, west of the present Beauport Park Golf Course.

Henry Thomsett's son Harold offered to show the author his father's underground hideout. Positioned on the edge of the wood, near to a footpath, the hideout has over the years, gradually collapsed and silted up. A nearby maple tree still has the aerial cable running up its trunk. The site was excavated to ascertain the method of construction employed.

The ceiling and the walls were all made up of corrugated iron and timber, apart from two small sections where bricks were used for walls. After removing the collapsed ceiling it was discovered that the main chamber had a concrete pit at its base. This measures six feet long, four feet wide and one and a half feet deep. This would have no doubt have had the radio set sitting on a table, along with a chair for the operator positioned inside of it. The

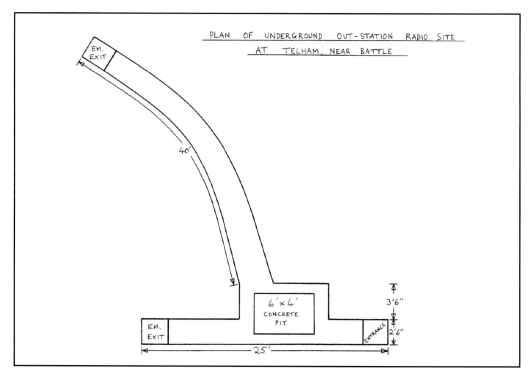

49. Excavation of the Telham site revealed a concrete pit to be the base of the hideout. Tree roots are the only thing keeping the roof of the hideout together.

50. Looking along the longest emergency exit tunnel. This was cut into a soft seam of sandstone.

51. The authors daughters, Kayleigh (left) and Danielle (right), pointing to the line of embedded aerial wire from Mr Thompsett's hideout that runs up the trunk of this tree. The actual aerial was made of copper and had a span of about eight feet, positioned up in the top branches of the tree. Parts of the aerial wire can still be seen where they have popped out with the growth of the trees trunk.

pit had its own drainage gully and was dug deep enough for a person to stand upright in the hideout, in fact this is the only area within the hideout where this would have been possible. Two emergency exit tunnels ran out from this main chamber, the longest being 40 feet long. Both terminated in an earth-covered wooden hatch.

West Sussex

The author is indebted to Denis Allman for imparting the following information about radio operators in the Chichester and Arundel area.

Each radio operator was equipped with one transmitter, code sheets, a small amount of emergency food rations and a revolver with ammunition. Although not issued with Home Guard uniforms, the radio operators and associated personnel were all classified as members of the 13th Platoon of the Home Guard. Each man had to sign the Official Secrets Act.

All the radios were hidden, often within underground hideouts, running the aerial up a tree so as to gain the height that was needed.

A Major Fraser from Sevenoaks in Kent was in charge of the south-eastern region. He wore civilian clothes and had a car along with a driver, equipped with a radio transmitter.

Denis Allman's father Ernest Allman, himself a radio operator, was responsible for the radio operators in the Chichester and Arundel area. He was issued with a special pass that allowed him complete freedom of movement, even in restricted areas. His own transmitter was located at the family home 'Elmstead' in the parish of Birdham, south of Chichester. Initially it was in a semi-underground air raid shelter. Later it was moved to a secret room which had been built into the end of a large wooden shed within the garden. The only access to this room was by a door disguised as a side panel that could only be opened by lifting a hidden latch with a knitting needle. The aerial for the transmitter went up into an elm tree in the garden. Denis himself was involved not only as a messenger between the local out-stations for his father but also in the capacity of a spy. Being a part-time member of the fire service he was able to carry out these duties without suspicion.

Denis Allman also remembers other members of the organisation. Mr Hoskins, a fisherman from West Wittering, was enrolled as a lookout/spy to report enemy movements around Chichester Harbour. A Mr Williams, who was a tractor driver for W A Aylwin of Sidlesham, became a radio operator. His radio was sited in a marshy area with trees at Church Norton, just outside of Selsey. He was originally a member of the Home Guard which, on his leaving to join the Special Duties Organisation, created speculation as to what his war effort had become.

Walter Langmead, a well known farmer from Runcton, was a radio operator for a short while. The radio set was hidden in the loft of a barn, just off the main road to Pagham. On his leaving the organisation the radio was moved to South Mundham. Its new operator was Admiral Palmer (retired). The radio was sited within a large tank under the floorboards of a disused chapel, its only entrance being a trapdoor. The tank was installed by Canadian Royal Engineers. Denis remembers on one occasion visiting Admiral Palmer only to find him sitting beside the radio with wellington boots on because of severe flooding. The Royal Engineers were called back to rectify this problem.

Another radio operator was Frank Campbell, a retired electrical engineer from Manchester who owned the 'Warming Pan' restaurant, just outside Arundel on the A27 (now known as 'Howard's Carvery'). Frank Campbell's radio was sited in an underground chamber amongst a clump of trees on the opposite side of the road to his restaurant. To get to his radio set he had to go down into the cellar. Underneath a slate shelf, a small section of the cellar wall was actually mounted on rails via ball bearings, and when a six inch nail was pushed into a certain crack within this wall, a locking catch lifted, allowing the wall to be pushed in along these rails. Once beyond this wall, Frank Campbell would crawl along a tunnel that ran under the main A27 road, and finally enter the underground chamber. Both the tunnel and chamber were built by Canadian engineers.

Within a short space of time a major problem occurred at the site, as the road started to subside where the tunnel ran under it. The local authorities, not knowing about the tunnel, were puzzled by what was happening. Denis Allman, his father and a Canadian sergeant from the engineers visited the site to inspect the damage underground. It was decided to abandon the tunnel, at which point the engineers filled it in to make it safe and prevent any more sinkage of the road.

After this the underground chamber for the radio was upgraded by sinking a large tank similar to the one used under the chapel at South Munden. Former West Sussex scout patrol member Les Hawkins remembers laying an electrical cable for Frank Campbell, from his underground hideout over to a nearby flint wall. Connected to the cable was a two-way intercom which was hidden among some ivy growing up the wall. In the event of a German invasion the vicar would have used the intercom, at specified times, to relay any information he had gained about local German troop movements back to Frank Campbell, who in turn would have coded and transmitted the details. Although mentioned in 'The Last Ditch' by David Lampe, the exact location of the site along with the identity of its radio operator has, up until now, remained unknown.

52. Ernest Allman, himself a radio operator and responsible for the other radio operators in the Arundel and Chichester area.

53. Denis Allman, acted as a messenger between the various radio operators for his father.

Four miles north of Frank Campbell's hideout, another radio was positioned on Bury Hill near Bury in a small underground hideout among some trees just off the A29 road. Former West Sussex scout patrol member Sidney Gaston remembers constructing this hideout. Its operator was Reginald Pitts, already listed as a member of the Warningcamp Patrol concerned with sabotage activities. He was evidently classed as a very trustworthy person, and this is an example of a rare situation where a man belonged to both the Special Duties Organisation and an Auxiliary Unit patrol.

The only other known radio operator is a Mr Baron, a farmer in Clapham, who kept his transmitter hidden in the back of his bull pen: probably the best-guarded radio set in Sussex!

While the Special Duties Organisation were busy setting up a communications network, key GPO personnel were briefed on how to sabotage the telephone system if the Germans invaded. Former telephone mobile lineman Dennis Thompsett explained how it would have been his job to disconnect and remove the ringer machines in the telephone exchange which enabled a caller to connect with the number dialled. On receiving the go-ahead from the local area military commander, he also had to put an axe through the cable chamber where marked with white paint. He would then go on to the next exchange, trying to keep one step ahead of the Germans. As this kind of work would move him out of his area, he was issued with a special document to get money from army sources.

Zero Stations

The purpose of a Zero Station was to receive coded information from the many out-stations in the surrounding area, passing on the details via a direct phone line to the Special Duties headquarters at Hannington Hall, Wiltshire. Sussex had three of these underground Zero Stations, one in a wood in Heathfield, East Sussex, and two in West Sussex: the better-known of these was in the grounds of Wakehurst Place, near Ardingly, and the other near Shipley, about ten miles west of Haywards Heath, close to the A272 road. All three were built to the same plan, the only variant being the length of the emergency exit tunnel.

The women operatives of these Zero Stations were members of the ATS with Beatrice Temple as their Senior Commander. Miss Temple would often visit the underground sites around the country to check that the women were all right and generally monitor how the system was working. The Royal Corps of Signals were in charge of checking and maintaining the radio equipment.

Many years after the war, Beatrice Temple, a former Mayoress of Lewes, returned to the Heathfield wood that she had visited many times during the sites' operational years, to try to locate the switch that opened the entrance hatch. This switch was concealed behind a hinged piece of bark on a tree. When operated, the switch released the entrance hatch some 30ft away. However, despite a long search, no trace of the switch or indeed the underground Zero Station could be found.

With the Heathfield site gone and the one in the grounds of Wakehurst Place sealed up, the Zero Station at Shipley was the only accessible and complete site for investigation. Taking into account that the basic design of each was the same, the information gained at Shipley can be related to the other two Sussex sites in respect of size and shape.

Built on a solid concrete base with corrugated iron arched across to form its roof, the hideout resembles, like many of the sabotage patrol hideouts, an underground Nissan hut. Entrance was gained by lifting a concealed earth-covered wooden trapdoor. At Shipley this had a counterbalance weight to assist opening. With the trapdoor open, a wooden ladder led down the entrance shaft, which opened out into a small room containing explosives and ammunition. This room was made to appear as if it were the only one, giving no indication of the main chamber, behind one of its walls, containing all the radio equipment. A system of shelves and carefully-stacked boxes hid the 5ft high door leading to this main chamber.

When a secret catch was lifted, a section of the shelving moved out of the way, allowing the door to be opened.

Along with the radio equipment, the main chamber contained a small table with chairs, bunk beds, spare batteries with a generator to recharge them and a good supply of food. The batteries were used for powering the radio equipment and a simple lighting arrangement.

The other end of the main chamber led into another small room which contained a chemical toilet, a drain in the floor, storage space and the entrance to the emergency exit tunnel. The three feet wide emergency exit tunnel was 16 feet long and terminated by opening out into a square concrete structure that had an earth covered wooden hatch above it concealing its existence.

Fresh air was supplied into the hideout by two one foot diameter asbestos pipes. One was positioned just off the floor and the other just below the roof. They ran along from the main chamber through the small end room until coming to the surface disguised as the holes of a badger sett. In fact when the site was visited in 1994 a badger had adopted part of the hideout as its home.

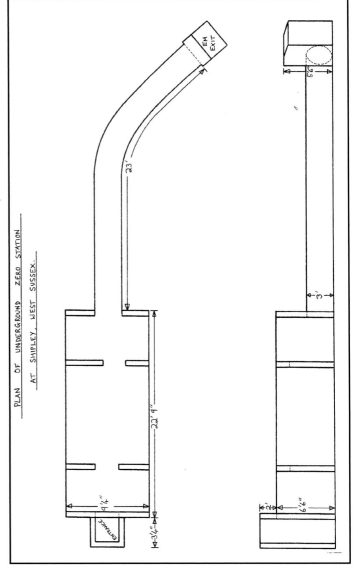

54. Inside the underground zero-station at Shipley. Now empty of its radio equipment but retaining enough features to identify its original use. Beyond the doorway is the hideouts entrance shaft.

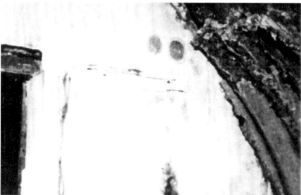

55. Although the wires have gone evidence of where they ran around the hideout can still be seen on the walls. The route of the wires shown probably led up to a couple of junction boxes now just bare circles on the whitewashed wall.

56. Groove cut out of an oak trees bark for the Shipley zero stations aerial wire to be hidden in. The bark would have been put back into the groove and fixed in position.

57. View of the hideout as you enter its main chamber from the entrance shaft end. To the left of the doorway are the two ventilation pipes. The shelf in between supported either a manual or diesel generator to be used when more fresh air was needed. A facility none of the sabotage side of the auxiliary units hideouts had. Beyond the doorway the start of the emergency exit tunnel can be seen.

58. Looking along the emergency exit tunnel. The wooden frame would have had a door attached to it and in turn this door had the chemical toilet fixed on to it.

Stand Down

Members of the Special Duties Organisation were informed of the decision to stand down their section of the Auxiliary Units by the following letter from the General Commander-in-Chief H E Franklyn:

```
Letter from General Sir Harold Franklyn, K.C.B., D.S.O., M.C. Commander-in-Chief
Home Forces To Commander, G.H.Q.; Auxiliary Units.

SECRET
HF/1267/G(SD)

The Commander, G.H.Q. Auxiliary Units

It had been decided by the War Office that, in view of the shortage of manpower
and the fact that the danger of invasion has receded, it is no longer possible
to retain the Special Duties organsation.

I realise that each member of the organisation from the first invasion days be-
ginning in 1940 voluntarily undertook a hazardous role which required both skill
and courage, well knowing that the very nature of their work would allow of no
public recognition.

This organsiation, founded on the keeness and patriotism of selected civilians
of all grades, has been in a position through its constant and thorough training
to furnish accurate information of raids or invasion instantly to military head-
quarters throughout the country. The fact that neither invasion nor raids have
in fact taken place does not detract in any way from the value of this work.

In recent days while our own invasion forces were concentrating, an additional
heavy burden was placed on those of you responsible for the maintenance of good
security, to ensure that the enemy was denied foreknowledge of our plans and
preparations. The Security Reports regularly provided by Special Duties have
proved of invaluable assistance to our security staffs.

As no public recognition can be given for this job so well done, it is my wish
that a copy of this letter be sent to all members of the Special Duties organisa-
tion as my own acknowledgement of the value and efficiency of their work.

(Signed) H.E. Franklyn
General Commander-in-Chief
4th July, 1944.
```

The latter part of the letter indicates the spies within the Special Duties Section were to be put to good use monitoring whether people were leaking information about the build-up of troops and equipment prior to the Normandy landings.

From the date at the bottom left of the letter it can be seen this stand down order was issued twenty one weeks before the Auxiliary Unit Patrols received their own order.

BIBLIOGRAPHY

OPERATION SEA LION
by Peter Fleming
HART - DAVIS. 1957

THE LAST DITCH
by David Lampe
CASSELL, LONDON. 1968

WEREWOLF - THE STORY OF THE NAZI RESISTANCE MOVEMENT
by Charles Whiting
LEO COOPER, LONDON. 1972

OPERATION SEALION
by Richard Cox
THORNTON - COX Ltd. 1974

INVASION - THE GERMAN INVASION OF ENGLAND JULY 1940
by Kenneth Macksey
ARMS AND ARMOUR PRESS. 1980

THE SECRET WAR OF CHARLES FRASER-SMITH
by Gerald Mcknight And Sandy Lesberg
MICHAEL JOSEPH, LONDON. 1981

HAILSHAM AT WAR
by Hailsham History Group Centre For Continuing Education
UNIVERSITY OF SUSSEX. 1986

AND ALL THE KINGS MEN
by Gordon Stevens
CHAPPMAN PUBLISHING LTD. 1990

KENT AND EAST SUSSEX UNDERGROUND
by Kent Underground Research Group
MERESBOROUGH BOOKS. 1991

THE MARCH ON LONDON
by Charles Whiting
LEO COOPER, LONDON. 1992

MP Middleton Press

OLVING THE ULTIMATE RAIL ENCYCLOPEDIA

Easebourne Lane, Midhurst, West Sussex.
GU29 9AZ   Tel:01730 813169

www.middletonpress.co.uk   email:info@middletonpress.co.uk
A-978 0 906520   B- 978 1 873793   C- 978 1 901706   D-978 1 904474   E - 978 1 906008

aveny to Merthyr C 91 8
tillery and Ebbw Vale Lines D 84 5
llows - Branch Line to A 62 8
 - Branch Lines to A 11 6
ver to Southampton A 82 6
- Branch Lines around A 64 2
urton - Branch Line to B 95 4
rd - Steam to Eurostar B 67 1
to Dover A 48 2
ian Narrow Gauge D 04 3
mouth - BL around D 42 5
bury to Rugby D 91 3

 Street to Uxbridge D 90 6
to Llandudno E 87 1
ury to Birmingham D 27 2
ury to Cheltenham E 63 5
or to Portmadoc E 72 7
ng to Southend C 80 2
outh to Pwllheli E 53 6
 - Branch Lines around D 50 0
Green Park to Bristol C 36 9
to Evercreech Junction A 60 4
rd to Wellingborough D 31 9
ngham to Wolverhampton E 25 3
hley to Cambridge D 94 4
hley to Rugby E 07 9
in - Branch Lines around B 83 1
nemouth to Evercreech Jn A 46 8
nemouth to Weymouth A 57 4
n to Neath D 43 2
n to Newport D 16 6
n to Newtown E 06 2
ton to Eastbourne A 16 1
ton to Worthing A 03 1
ley South to Rochester B 23 7
sgrove to Birmingham B 87 6
sgrove to Gloucester D 73 9
el - A railtour of his achievements D 74 6
 - Branch Line to B 29 9
ham to Evercreech Junction B 68 0

ridge to Ely D 55 5
erbury - Branch Lines around B 58 9
ff to Dowlais (Cae Harris) E 47 5
ff to Swansea E 42 0
sle to Hawick E 85 7
arthen to Fishguard E 66 6
ham & Tattenham Corner B 25 1
d and Yeovil - BLs around C 30 7
ng Cross to Dartford A 75 8
ng Cross to Orpington A 96 3
dar - Branch Line to B 90 9
enham to Andover C 43 7
enham to Redditch D 81 4
ester to Portsmouth A 14 7
am Junction to Beckenham Jn B 36 7
ury Mortimer - BLs around E 18 5
don & Portishead - BLs to D 18 0
el Stephens - His Empire D 62 3
ett to South Shields E 57 4
wall Narrow Gauge D 56 2
s and Vale of Rheidol E 65 9
en Arms to Llandeilo E 35 2
en Arms to Wellington E 33 8
ley to Littlehampton A 34 5
r - Branch Lines around C 26 0
don to East Grinstead B 48 0
al Palace and Catford Loop B 87 1
us Narrow Gauge E 13 0

gton - Leamside - Newcastle E 28 4
gton to Newcastle D 98 2
rd to Sittingbourne B 34 3
ent Valley - Branch Line to the D 06 7
n Narrow Gauge E 09 3
t to Banbury D 02 9
t to Swindon C 84 0
t to Winchester C 13 0
& Somerset Narrow Gauge D 76 0

Douglas - Laxey - Ramsey E 75 8
Douglas to Peel C 88 8
Douglas to Port Erin C 55 0
Douglas to Ramsey D 39 5
Dover to Ramsgate A 78 9
Dublin Northwards in the 1950s E 31 4
Dunstable - Branch Lines to E 27 7

E
Ealing to Slough C 42 0
East Cornwall Mineral Railways D 22 7
East Croydon to Three Bridges A 53 6
Eastern Spain Narrow Gauge E 56 7
East Grinstead - Branch Lines to A 07 9
East London - Branch Lines of C 44 4
East London Line B 80 0
East of Norwich - Branch Lines E 69 7
Effingham Junction - BLs around A 74 1
Ely to Norwich C 90 1
Enfield Town & Palace Gates - BL to D 32 6
Epsom to Horsham A 30 7
Eritrean Narrow Gauge E 38 3
Euston to Harrow & Wealdstone C 89 5
Exeter to Barnstaple B 15 2
Exeter to Newton Abbot C 49 9
Exeter to Tavistock B 69 5
Exmouth - Branch Lines to B 00 8

F
Fairford - Branch Line to A 52 9
Falmouth, Helston & St. Ives - BL to C 74 1
Fareham to Salisbury A 67 3
Faversham to Dover B 05 3
Felixstowe & Aldeburgh - BL to D 20 3
Fenchurch Street to Barking C 20 8
Festiniog - 50 yrs of enterprise C 83 3
Festiniog 1946-55 E 01 7
Festiniog in the Fifties B 68 8
Festiniog in the Sixties B 91 6
Finsbury Park to Alexandra Palace C 02 8
Frome to Bristol B 77 0

G
Gloucester to Bristol D 35 7
Gloucester to Cardiff D 66 1
Gosport - Branch Lines around A 36 9
Greece Narrow Gauge D 72 2

H
Hampshire Narrow Gauge D 36 4
Harrow to Watford D 14 2
Hastings to Ashford A 37 6
Hawkhurst - Branch Line to A 66 6
Hayling - Branch Line to A 12 3
Hay-on-Wye - Branch Lines around D 92 0
Haywards Heath to Seaford A 28 4
Hemel Hempstead - Branch Lines to D 88 3
Henley, Windsor & Marlow - BL to C77 2
Hereford to Newport D 54 8
Hertford and Hatfield - BLs around E 58 1 6
Hertford Loop E 71 0
Hexham to Carlisle D 75 3
Hitchin to Peterborough D 07 4
Holborn Viaduct to Lewisham A 81 9
Horsham - Branch Lines to A 02 4
Huntingdon - Branch Line to A 93 2

I
Ilford to Shenfield C 97 0
Ilfracombe - Branch Line to B 21 3
Industrial Rlys of the South East A 09 3
Ipswich to Saxmundham C 41 3
Isle of Wight Lines - 50 yrs C 12 3

K
Kent Narrow Gauge C 45 1
Kidderminster to Shrewsbury E 10 9
Kingsbridge - Branch Line to C 98 7
Kings Cross to Potters Bar E 62 9
Kingston & Hounslow Loops A 83 3
Kingswear - Branch Line to C 17 8

L
Lambourn - Branch Line to C 70 3
Launceston & Princetown - BL to C 19 2
Lewisham to Dartford A 92 5
Lines around Wimbledon B 75 6

Liverpool Street to Chingford D 01 2
Liverpool Street to Ilford C 34 5
Llandeilo to Swansea E 46 8
London Bridge to Addiscombe B 20 6
London Bridge to East Croydon A 58 1
Longmoor - Branch Lines to A 41 3
Looe - Branch Line to C 22 2
Lowestoft - Branch Lines around E 40 6
Ludlow to Hereford E 14 7
Lydney - Branch Lines around E 26 0
Lyme Regis - Branch Line to A 45 1
Lynton - Branch Line to B 04 6

M
Machynlleth to Barmouth E 54 3
March - Branch Lines around B 09 1
Marylebone to Rickmansworth D 49 4
Melton Constable to Yarmouth Beach E 03 1
Midhurst - Branch Lines of E 78 9
Mitcham Junction Lines B 01 5
Mitchell & company C 59 8
Monmouth - Branch Lines to E 20 8
Monmouthshire Eastern Valleys D 71 5
Moretonhampstead - BL to C 27 7
Moreton-in-Marsh to Worcester D 26 5
Mountain Ash to Neath D 80 7

N
Newbury to Westbury C 66 6
Newcastle to Hexham D 69 2
Newport (IOW) - Branch Lines to A 26 0
Newquay - Branch Lines to C 71 0
Newton Abbot to Plymouth C 60 4
Newtown to Aberystwyth E 41 3
North East German Narrow Gauge D 44 9
Northern France Narrow Gauge C 75 8
Northern Spain Narrow Gauge E 83 3
North London Line B 94 7
North Woolwich - BLs around C 65 9

O
Ongar - Branch Line to E 05 5
Oswestry - Branch Lines around E 60 4
Oswestry to Whitchurch E 81 9
Oxford to Bletchley D 57 9
Oxford to Moreton-in-Marsh D 15 9

P
Paddington to Ealing C 37 6
Paddington to Princes Risborough C 81 9
Padstow - Branch Line to B 54 1
Peterborough to Kings Lynn E 32 1
Plymouth - BLs around B 98 5
Plymouth to St. Austell C 63 5
Pontypool to Mountain Ash D 65 4
Pontypridd to Port Talbot E 86 4
Porthmadog 1954-94 - BL around B 31 2
Portmadoc 1923-46 - BL around B 13 8
Portsmouth to Southampton A 31 4
Portugal Narrow Gauge E 67 3
Potters Bar to Cambridge D 70 8
Princes Risborough - Branch Lines to D 05 0
Princes Risborough to Banbury C 85 7

R
Reading to Basingstoke B 27 5
Reading to Didcot C 79 6
Reading to Guildford A 47 5
Redhill to Ashford A 73 4
Return to Blaenau 1970-82 C 64 2
Rhymney and New Tredegar Lines E 48 2
Rickmansworth to Aylesbury D 61 6
Romania & Bulgaria Narrow Gauge E 23 9
Romneyrail C 32 1
Ross-on-Wye - Branch Lines around E 30 7
Ruabon to Barmouth E 84 0
Rugby to Birmingham E 37 6
Ryde to Ventnor A 19 2

S
Salisbury to Westbury B 39 8
Saxmundham to Yarmouth C 69 7
Saxony Narrow Gauge D 47 0
Seaton & Sidmouth - Branch Lines to A 95 6
Selsey - Branch Line to A 04 8
Sheerness - Branch Line to B 16 2

Shrewsbury - Branch Line to A 86 4
Shrewsbury to Chester E 70 3
Shrewsbury to Ludlow E 21 5
Shrewsbury to Newtown E 29 1
Sierra Leone Narrow Gauge D 28 9
Sirhowy Valley Line E 12 3
Sittingbourne to Ramsgate A 90 1
Slough to Newbury C 56 7
South African Two-foot gauge E 51 2
Southampton to Bournemouth A 42 0
Southend & Southminster - B Ls to E 76 5
Southern France Narrow Gauge C 47 5
South London Line B 46 6
Southwold - Branch Line to A 15 4
Spalding - Branch Lines around E 52 9
St Albans to Bedford D 08 1
St. Austell to Penzance C 67 3
Steaming through the Isle of Wight A 56 7
Steaming through West Hants A 69 7
Stourbridge to Wolverhampton E 16 1
St. Pancras to Barking D 68 5
St. Pancras to Folkestone E 88 8
St. Pancras to St. Albans C 78 9
Stratford-upon-Avon to Birmingham D 77 7
Stratford-upon-Avon to Cheltenham C 25 3
Surrey Narrow Gauge C 87 1
Sussex Narrow Gauge C 68 0
Swanley to Ashford B 45 9
Swansea to Carmarthen E 59 8
Swindon to Bristol C 96 3
Swindon to Gloucester D 46 3
Swindon to Newport D 30 2
Swiss Narrow Gauge C 94 9

T
Talyllyn - 50 years C 39 0
Taunton to Barnstaple B 60 2
Taunton to Exeter C 82 6
Tavistock to Plymouth B 88 6
Tenterden - Branch Line to A 21 5
Three Bridges to Brighton A 35 2
Tilbury Loop C 86 4
Tiverton - Branch Lines around C 62 8
Tivetshall to Beccles D 41 8
Tonbridge to Hastings A 44 4
Torrington - Branch Lines to B 37 4
Towcester - Branch Lines around E 39 0
Tunbridge Wells - Branch Lines to A 32 1

U
Upwell - Branch Line to B 64 0

V
Victoria to Bromley South A 98 7
Vivarais Revisited E 08 6

W
Wantage - Branch Line to D 25 8
Wareham to Swanage - 50 yrs D 09 8
Waterloo to Windsor A 54 3
Waterloo to Woking A 38 3
Watford to Leighton Buzzard D 45 6
Welshpool to Llanfair E 49 9
Wenford Bridge to Fowey C 09 3
Westbury to Bath B 55 8
Westbury to Taunton C 76 5
West Cornwall Mineral Railways D 48 7
West Croydon to Epsom B 08 4
West German Narrow Gauge D 93 7
West London - Branch Lines of C 50 5
West London Line B 84 8
West Wiltshire - Branch Lines of D 12 8
Weymouth - Branch Lines around A 65 9
Willesden Junction to Richmond B 71 8
Wimbledon to Beckenham C 58 1
Wimbledon to Epsom B 62 6
Wimborne - Branch Lines around A 97 0
Wisbech 1800-1901 C 93 2
Wisbech - Branch Lines around C 01 7
Witham & Kelvedon - BLs around E 82 6
Woking to Alton A 59 8
Woking to Portsmouth A 25 3
Woking to Southampton A 55 0
Wolverhampton to Shrewsbury E 44 4
Worcester to Birmingham D 97 5
Worcester to Hereford D 38 8
Worthing to Chichester A 06 2

Y
Yeovil - 50 yrs change C 38 3
Yeovil to Dorchester A 76 5
Yeovil to Exeter A 91 8